THE WORD FOR US

The Gospels of John and Mark
Epistles to the Romans and the Galatians

Restated in
Inclusive Language

by Joann Haugerud

published by
Coalition on Women and Religion
Seattle

Published by
   Coalition on Women and Religion
   4759 15th Avenue, Northeast
   Seattle, Washington 98105

First Edition   August 1977
   Second printing   November 1977
   Third printing   July 1980
   Fourth printing   May 1981

Library of Congress catalog card number: 77-83418

ISBN: 0-9603042-3-1

PRINTED IN THE UNITED STATES OF AMERICA

--for all our sisters and brothers--

Contents

INTRODUCTION

When Jesus called Peter, Andrew, James, and John, and invited them to become (according to the King James and other versions) "fishers of men," did Jesus mean that they would set out to catch male humans only? Or were women to be included? If the former, then Christianity is really for men only and women would do well to shun it. But if Jesus meant to include all people in the invitation to a new way of living, and there is ample evidence that he did, then the correct contemporary English translation of these words is "fishers of women and men." *(Mark 1.17)*

This is what I believe, and this belief is why **The Word For Us** came into being.

Every translation is based on both literal meanings of the original language and implications seen in the new language by the translator. My disagreement with previous translators is that they have clung to the literal where it contains exclusively masculine language, while freely interpreting other words according to their various insights. Some have even added to the masculinity by changing the Holy Spirit from the neuter in Greek to masculine in English, calling it "he." *(John 14.26)* For these reasons I do not believe that I differ radically from other translators in method, but our resulting word choices are different.

Along with including both women and men as hearers of the word, I am concerned that the language describing God has been heavily masculine in the past, with the result that people can scarcely avoid thinking of God as a male person. Language affects us that way. But, logically and existentially, it is impossible that the source and sustainer of all being could be of only one sex. Thus, the masculine language must be removed from descriptive phrases relating to God.

When language is corrected so that it pointedly includes all people, and frees the image of God from human limitations, something mysterious happens. The message takes on a breadth and intensity that was not noticed before. Reading scripture becomes an experience in wholeness, and this experience is the real motive for publishing **The Word For Us** now. My hope is that a taste of wholeness will encourage others to work toward providing a whole Bible in inclusive language. I am continuing to work on restating additional scripture, and I hope others will too.

Quite early in the research and writing of **The Word For Us**, I developed a rationale for the kind of language to be used. It has not changed materially over time, and I include it here as a point of reference.

1. Maleness and femaleness are physiological properties.
2. God, being spirit, is neither male nor female.
3. People collectively are both male and female.
4. A specific person is either male or female.
5. A non-specific person must not exclude either sex.
6. Jesus, while walking the earth, was a human male, but his maleness was not an essential property of his mission; rather it was a convenience in that time and place.
7. The concept of Messiah or Christ is neither male nor female; the expected one was unknown as to human characteristics.
8. The risen Christ, being no longer confined to a physical body, is neither male nor female.
9. It is biologically impossible for a person to have only male ancestors.

Based on this rationale, God has no pronoun references in this book, nor are any metaphors used which might seem to indicate that God is confined to one sex. Gone are the lords, fathers, kings, and kingdoms. No fixed substitutes can be listed, as each instance had to be dealt with in its context and in a manner that best expressed the idea to be conveyed. I found new clarity in some passages, and the process of working out meanings expanded my understanding of the metaphor. I hope it will do the same for the reader.

For example, to find out what fatherhood meant, read John 5.18-23 and John 8.37-47. It becomes clear that Jesus, speaking to people in his own time and place, made use of the prevailing concept of fatherhood to explain something about God and people. But since that concept is not part of our culture, we need to use other words. Fatherhood, for the Judeans, represented their ancestry, culture, who they were, and what they were like—their whole being. Jesus tried to show them that his parentage, heritage, and being came from God, and further suggested that people should not claim ancestry that they are not willing to emulate.

When Jesus claimed to be a Child of God, he was recognizing God as the source of his being and was willing to do what that relationship required.

Jesus more often called himself "Child of Humanity" ("Son of Man" in other English versions) signifying that he claimed kinship and identity with the whole human race. Jesus identified himself with humanity rather than connecting only to ancestors of his own nation or religion.

I tried several phrases to express this concept, and kept returning to "Child of Humanity" and "Humanity's Child" as being less imperfect than other possibilities. But readers of the manuscript have expressed dissatisfaction with the "child" part of it, because child seems to indicate a little person rather than a grown up offspring or descendant. A suggested substitute was "Human Being" which does mean the same as "Child of Humanity." You may wish to try out other non-sexist combinations for yourself. I continue to prefer "Child of Humanity" because of its sound and for the symbolism of generational continuity. A child of humanity is not just an individual but is human, reproduced after its own kind. Jesus claimed this connection with the rest of us children of humanity, and I treasure that.

The points in this book where I depart farthest from historical accuracy are the instances of people quoting Old Testament sources. For example, Paul did not always mention Sarah with Abraham, nor quote prophecy in inclusive language; but Sarah was truly involved in the ancestry, and prophecy is for all people, so I think it is more important to be inclusive and truthful than to quote Paul literally.

Throughout the text, to alleviate the ponderous weight of masculine pronouns, I have often repeated a person's name instead of using a pronoun. The naming also clarifies some passages where a diagram was required to figure out which he was saying what to which other he.

In addition to deviations for inclusiveness, there are other words that may fall unfamiliarly upon your ear: "Judean" for "Jew," "outsiders" or "other nations" for "Gentiles," and "slave" for "servant" in some places. These are reclamations of the literal Greek from which others had deviated before me.

My publisher, the *Coalition on Women and Religion,* has as one of its goals, to "examine and reinterpret scripture and theology from the feminist perspective." I am grateful that they chose to publish **The Word For Us** as part of their ongoing concern for women and women authors, and I wish to thank members of the Coalition who have been encouraging to me throughout the project.

In addition to the Coalition, members of Women in Ministry, the Liberation Church, and the Tuesday group, gave me strength and incentive to bring this book to publication. We believe that our interlocking communities need and want it.

Other people were supportive in concrete ways with loans and gifts to the Coalition on Women and Religion to cover initial costs of publication. And still others were helpful to me by reading the manuscript at various stages and commenting on it. A few precious souls are in all these categories.

Following are some helpful folks, listed in reverse alphabetical order: Barbara VanArk Wilson, Lois Wentzel, Doris Warbington, Marie Van Bronkhorst, Ruth Schilperoort, Grace Reed Rowan, Rosemary Powers, Rev. Christine Morton, Jessie Kinnear, Shirlie Kaplan, Mary Jane Jones, L. Faye Ignatius and the National Ministries of the American Baptist Church, Rev. Marie Fortune, Sr. Mary Fleming, Jan Cate, Jane Brown, Eleanor Bilimoria, and Esther Brolin Bailey.

Joann Haugerud
Seattle, June 1977

The Gospel According to John

Chapter I

[1]IN THE BEGINNING was the Word, and the Word was with God, and the Word was God. [2]The Word existed from the beginning with God. [3]All things were made through the Word, and nothing that was made was made without the Word. [4]In the Word was life, and that life was humanity's light. [5]The light shines in the darkness, and the darkness does not overcome it.

[6]A certain man, named John, was sent from God. [7]John came as a witness, that through his testimony concerning the light, all people might believe. [8]John was not the light, but came to be a witness concerning the light.

[9]It was the true light which enlightens every person that was coming into the world. [10]The light already was in the world, and the world was made through that light, but the world did not know it. [11]The light came to its own place and its own people would not receive it. [12]But to all who did receive that light, to all who believed in the embodiment of the light, was given the power to become children of God; [13]children born, not of blood, nor of the will of the flesh, nor of the will of woman and man, but of God.

[14]And the Word became flesh and lived among us, full of grace and truth. We saw the glory of the Word, glory as of a unique Child of God. [15]John witnessed to the Word, and cried, "This is the one of whom I said, 'The one who comes after me ranks before me and was before me.'"

[16]From this fullness we have all received grace upon grace. [17]For the law was given through Moses, but grace and truth came through Jesus Christ. [18]No one has ever seen God. But the beloved of God, who lives in God's bosom, makes God known.

[19]This is the testimony of John. When the Judeans sent priests and Levites from Jerusalem to ask, "Who are you?" [20]John confessed, did not deny, but affirmed, "I am not the Christ."

21Then they asked, "What then? Are you Elijah?"

John said, "I am not."

"Are you the prophet?"

And John said, "No."

22They said then, "Who are you? Let us have an answer for those who sent us. What do you say about yourself?"

23John said, "I am the voice of one crying in the wilderness, 'Make God's road straight,' as the prophet Isaiah said." *(Is 40.3)*

24Now they had been sent from the Pharisees. 25And they asked John, "Why then are you baptizing, if you are neither the Christ nor Elijah, nor the prophet?"

26John answered them, "I baptize in water, but among you stands one whom you do not know, 27the one who comes after me, the one whose sandal I am not worthy to untie."

28These things took place in Bethany beyond the Jordan, where John was baptizing. 29The next day John saw Jesus coming toward him, and said, "Look, there is the Lamb of God who takes away the sin of the world! 30This is the one of whom I said, 'After me comes one who will be before me, and was before me.' 31I myself did not know this person, but for this I came baptizing in water, that this one might be revealed to Israel."

32And John witnessed, saying, "I saw the Spirit descend as a dove from Heaven, and remain on him. 33I myself did not know who this was, but the one who sent me to baptize with water said to me, 'On whomever you see the Spirit descend and remain, this is the one who baptizes with the Holy Spirit.' 34And I have seen and have witnessed that this is the one who comes from God."

35The next day again John was standing with two of his disciples. 36Looking at Jesus as he walked, John said, "See, the Lamb of God!"

37The two disciples heard John say this, and they followed Jesus. 38Turning around, Jesus saw them following and said to them, "What do you seek?"

And they said, "Rabbi (which means teacher), where are you staying?"

39Jesus said to them, "Come and see."

They came and saw where he was staying, and they stayed with

Jesus that day, for it was about the tenth hour. [40]One of the two who heard John speak, and followed Jesus, was Andrew, the brother of Simon Peter. [41]Andrew first found his brother Simon, and said to him, "We have found the Messiah." (which means Christ)

[42]Andrew brought Simon to Jesus, who looked at him and said, "You are Simon son of John? You shall be called Cephas." (which means Peter in Greek, Rock in English)

[43]The next day Jesus decided to go to Galilee, and finding Philip, said to him, "Follow me."

[44]Now Philip was from Bethsaida, the city of Andrew and Peter. [45]Philip found Nathanael, and said to him, "We have found the one of whom Moses in the law and also the prophets wrote, Jesus, son of Joseph and Mary from Nazareth."

[46]Nathanael said to Philip, "Can anything good come out of Nazareth?"

Philip said, "Come and see."

[47]Jesus saw Nathanael coming toward him and said, "Look, an Israelite indeed, in whom is no guile!"

[48]Nathanael said to Jesus, "How do you know me?"

Jesus answered, "Before Philip called you, when you were under the fig tree, I saw you."

[49]Nathanael responded, "Rabbi, you are the chosen one of God! You are the ruler of Israel!"

[50]Jesus answered him, "Because I told you that I saw you under the fig tree, do you believe? You shall see greater things than these." [51]And Jesus continued, "Thus truly* I tell you, you will see heaven opened, and the angels of God going up and coming down upon the Child of Humanity."

Chapter II

[1]ON THE THIRD DAY there was a marriage at Cana in Galilee, and Mary the mother of Jesus was there; [2]Jesus and his disciples were also invited to the marriage. [3]When the wine failed, Mary said to Jesus, "They have no wine."

[4]And Jesus said to her, "O woman, what has that to do with

*Amen, amen, or truly, truly.

you or me? My time has not yet come."

⁵But Mary said to the servants, "Do whatever he tells you."

⁶Now six stone jars were standing there, for the Jewish rites of purification, each holding twenty or thirty gallons. ⁷Jesus said to them, "Fill the jars with water," and they filled them up to the brim.

⁸Then Jesus said, "Now draw some out, and take it to the steward of the feast." So they took it.

⁹When the steward of the feast tasted the water now become wine, and did not know where it came from (though the servants who had drawn the water knew), the steward called the bridegroom ¹⁰and said to him, "Everyone serves the good wine first, and when all have drunk freely, then the poor wine, but you have kept the good wine until now."

¹¹Jesus did this, the first of his signs, at Cana in Galilee, and demonstrated his glory. The disciples believed in him.

¹²After this Jesus went down to Capernaum with his mother, sisters, brothers, and disciples, and they stayed there for a few days.

¹³The Passover of the Judeans was about to begin and Jesus went up to Jerusalem. ¹⁴In the temple he found those who were selling oxen, sheep, and pigeons, and there the money changers sat. ¹⁵Then, making a whip of cords, Jesus drove them all, including sheep and oxen, out of the temple. He poured out the coins of the money changers and overturned their tables. ¹⁶And Jesus told those who sold pigeons, "Take these things away; you shall not make the house of God a house of business."

¹⁷His disciples remembered that it was written, "Zeal for your house will consume me." *(Ps 69.9)*

¹⁸The Judeans then said, "What sign have you to show us for doing these things?"

¹⁹Jesus answered them, "Destroy this temple, and in three days I will raise it up."

²⁰The Judeans then said, "It has taken forty-six years to build this temple, and will you raise it up in three days?"

²¹But Jesus was speaking of the temple of his body. ²²Therefore, when Jesus was raised from the dead, his disciples remem-

bered that he had said this, and they believed the scripture and the words Jesus had spoken.

²³While Jesus was in Jerusalem at the Passover feast, many put their trust in the name of Jesus (which means savior), from seeing the signs which he was doing. ²⁴But Jesus did not trust himself to them, ²⁵because he knew the world and needed no one to testify concerning human behavior. For Jesus himself knew what was in people.

Chapter III

¹NOW THERE WAS a man of the Pharisees, named Nicodemus, a ruler of the Judeans. ²This Nicodemus came to Jesus by night and said, "Rabbi, we know that you are a teacher come from God, for you could not do these signs that you do without God being with you."

³Jesus answered, "Thus truly I tell you, unless a person is born anew, he or she cannot comprehend the power of God."

⁴Nicodemus said to him, "How can a person be born when old? Can one enter a second time into the mother's womb and be born?"

⁵Jesus answered, "Thus truly I tell you, unless any one is born both of water and of spirit, one cannot enter into the realm of God. ⁶That which is born of the flesh is flesh, and that which is born of the spirit is spirit. ⁷Do not marvel that I said to you, 'You must be born anew.' ⁸The wind blows where it wills, and you hear the sound of it, but you do not know where it comes from or where it goes. So it is with everyone who is born of the spirit."*

⁹Nicodemus said to Jesus, "How can this be?"

¹⁰Jesus answered, "Are you a teacher of Israel and yet you do not understand this? ¹¹Thus truly I tell you, we speak of what we know, and bear witness to what we have seen, but you do not receive our testimony. ¹²If I have told you earthly things and you do not believe, how can you believe if I tell you heavenly things? ¹³No one has gone into heaven except the one who came from heaven, the Child of Humanity. ¹⁴And as Moses lifted up the serpent in the wilderness, so must Humanity's Child be lifted up, ¹⁵that every

*Greek word "pneuma" means both wind and spirit, thus making translation of this paragraph always uncertain.

5

one who trusts may have eternal life.''

[16]God loved the world, loved it so much that the beloved Child of God was given to the world, and all who trust in this unique being will never perish but have eternal life. [17]For God sent Jesus into the world, not to condemn the world, but that by this means the world might be saved. [18]All who trust in the Child of God are not judged. All who do not believe have already been judged, because they do not trust in the name of the one sent from God. [19]And this is the judgment, that the light came into the world, and people loved darkness rather than light, because their works were evil. [20]For all who do evil hate the light, and do not come to the light, because their evil works would be exposed. [21]But one who does the truth comes to the light that it may be seen clearly that these deeds have been done in God.

[22]After this Jesus and his disciples went into the land of Judea, and remained there and baptized. [23]John also was baptizing at Aenon near Salim, because there was plenty of water there, and people came and were baptized. [24]For John had not yet been put in prison.

[25]Now a discussion arose between John's disciples and a Judean over purifying. [26]And they came to John and said to him, ''Rabbi, the one who was with you beyond the Jordan, to whom you witnessed, is here baptizing, and all are coming to him.''

[27]John answered, ''No one can receive anything unless it is given from heaven. [28]You yourselves witnessed that I said, 'I am not the Christ,' but I have been sent before the Christ. [29]The one who has the bride is the bridegroom, but the friend of the bridegroom, who stands and hears him, rejoices greatly at the bridegroom's voice; therefore my joy has now been fulfilled. [30]Jesus must increase, but I must decrease.''

[31]The one who comes from above is above all; the one who is of the earth is the earth's, and of the earth speaks. The one who comes from heaven is over all, [32]testifying to what has been seen and heard, yet no one receives the testimony. [33]But all who do receive this testimony are witnesses that God is true. [34]The one whom God has sent speaks the words of God, for not by measure is the spirit given. [35]Like a parent God loves and gives all things into the hand

of the Child. [36]Any one who believes in the Child has eternal life; those who do not obey shall not see life, but the wrath of God remains upon them.

Chapter IV

[1]WHEN JESUS LEARNED that the Pharisees had heard of his making and baptizing more disciples than John, [2]although Jesus himself did not baptize, but only his disciples, [3]Jesus left Judea and departed again to Galilee. [4]He had to pass through Samaria, [5]and so came to a city of Samaria, called Sychar, near the field that Jacob gave to his son Joseph. [6]Jacob's well was there. So Jesus, wearied as he was with the journey, sat down beside the well. It was about the sixth hour.

[7]There came a woman of Samaria to draw water. Jesus said to her, "Give me a drink." [8]For his disciples had gone away into the city to buy food.

[9]The Samaritan woman said to him, "How is it that you, a Judean, ask a drink of me, a woman of Samaria?" For Judeans have no dealings with Samaritans.

[10]Jesus answered her, "If you knew the gift of God, and who it is that is saying to you, 'Give me a drink,' you would have asked and I would have given you living water."

[11]The woman said to him, "Sir, you have nothing to draw with and the well is deep; where do you get that living water? [12]Are you greater than our ancestors Jacob, Leah, and Rachel, who gave us the well and drank from it themselves, and their children, and their cattle?"

[13]Jesus said to her, "Everyone who drinks of this water will thirst again, [14]but all who drink of the water that I shall give will never thirst. The water that I give becomes in them a spring of water welling up to eternal life."

[15]The woman said to him, "Sir, give me this water, that I may not thirst, nor come here to draw."

[16]Jesus said to her, "Go, call your husband, and come here."

[17]The woman answered him, "I have no husband."

[18]Jesus said to her, "You are right in saying, 'I have no hus-

band,' for you have had five husbands, and he whom you now have is not your husband. You speak truthfully.''

[19]The woman said to him, "Sir, I perceive that you are a prophet. [20]Our ancestors worshiped on this mountain, and you say that in Jerusalem is the place where people ought to worship.''

[21]Jesus said to her, "Woman, believe me, the time is coming when neither on this mountain nor in Jerusalem will you worship God. [22]You worship what you do not know; we worship what we know, for salvation is from the Judeans. [23]But the time is coming, and now is, when true worshipers will worship God in spirit and truth, for such God seeks as worshipers. [24]God is spirit, and those who worship God must worship in spirit and truth.''

[25]The woman said to Jesus, "I know that the Messiah is coming (the one who is called Christ). When that one comes all things will be shown to us.''

[26]Jesus said to her, "I who speak to you am that one.''

[27]Just then his disciples returned and they marveled that Jesus was talking with a woman. But none said, "What do you wish?'' or "Why are you talking with her?''

[28]So the woman left her water jar, and went away into the city, and said to the people, [29]"Come, see a man who told me all that I ever did. Can this be the Christ?'' [30]Then they went out of the city and came to Jesus.

[31]Meanwhile the disciples urged Jesus, saying, "Rabbi, eat.''

[32]But Jesus said to them, "I have food to eat of which you do not know.''

[33]So the disciples said to one another, "Has anyone brought him food?''

[34]Jesus said to them, "My food is to do the will of the one who sent me, and to finish God's work. [35]Do you not say, 'There are yet four months, then comes the harvest'? Look, I tell you, lift up your eyes and see the fields already white for harvest. [36]Already the reaper receives wages and gathers fruit for eternal life, so that the planter and reaper may rejoice together. [37]For in this the word is true, 'One plants and another reaps.' [38]I sent you to reap that for which you did not labor; others have labored, and you have entered into their labor.''

[39]Many Samaritans from that city believed in Jesus because of the woman's testimony, "He told me all that I ever did." [40]So when the Samaritans came to Jesus, they asked him to stay with them, and he stayed there two days. [41]And many more believed because of what Jesus told them. [42]Then they said to the woman, "It is no longer only because of what you said that we believe; we have heard for ourselves and we know that this is truly the savior of the world."

[43]After the two days Jesus departed to Galilee, [44]and witnessed that prophets have no honor in their own country. [45]When Jesus came to Galilee, the Galileans welcomed him, having seen all the things that he had done in Jerusalem at the feast, for they too had gone to the feast.

[46]Jesus came again to Cana in Galilee, where he had made the water wine. And there was a certain royal official whose son was ill in Capernaum. [47]Hearing that Jesus had come from Judea to Galilee, this man went to Jesus and begged him to come down and heal his son, for he was at the point of death. [48]Jesus said to him, "Unless you see signs and wonders you will not believe."

[49]The official said to him, "Sir, come down before my child dies."

[50]Jesus said, "Go, your son will live."

The man believed the word that Jesus spoke to him and went his way. [51]As he was going, servants met him and said that the boy was alive. [52]So the official asked them at what time the child had begun to get better, and they said, "Yesterday at the seventh hour the fever left him."

[53]The father knew that was the hour when Jesus had told him, "Your son will live." Then he believed, along with the whole household.

[54]This was now the second sign that Jesus did, having come from Judea to Galilee.

Chapter V

[1]AFTER THIS there was a feast of the Judeans, and Jesus went up to Jerusalem.

[2]Now in Jerusalem by the Sheep Gate there is a pool, called in Hebrew Bethzatha, which has five porches. [3]In these lay a crowd of invalids, blind, lame, paralyzed, (waiting for the moving of the water; [4]for an angel went down at certain seasons into the pool, and troubled the water. Whoever stepped in first after the troubling of the water was healed of whatever disease she or he had.)* [5]One man was there who had been ill for thirty-eight years. [6]When Jesus saw him and knew that he had been lying there a long time, he said to him, "Do you want to be healed?"

[7]The sick man answered him, "Sir, I have no one to put me into the pool when the water is troubled, and while I am going another steps down before me."

[8]Jesus said to him, "Stand up, take your mat and walk."

[9]And immediately the man was healed, and picked up his mat and walked. That day was the sabbath.

[10]So the Judeans said to the man who was healed, "It is the sabbath, it is not lawful for you to carry your mat."

[11]But he answered them, "The man who healed me said to me, 'Take your mat and walk.'"

[12]They asked him, "Who said to you, 'Take your mat and walk'?"

[13]The one who had been healed did not know who it was. Jesus had withdrawn, for there was a crowd in the place. [14]Afterward, Jesus found him in the temple, and said to him, "See, you are well! Sin no more, that nothing worse befall you."

[15]The man went away and told the Judeans that it was Jesus who had healed him. [16]And this was why the Judeans persecuted Jesus, because he had done this on the sabbath. [17]But Jesus answered them, "The one from whom I descended is still working, and I work."

[18]This was why the Judeans sought all the more to kill Jesus, because he not only broke the sabbath but also claimed to be descended from God, making himself equal with God.

[19]Jesus answered them, "Thus truly I tell you, a child can do nothing independently, but only what the child sees a parent doing; for whatever parents do, their children do likewise. [20]For the parents love the child and demonstrate all that parents do. [21]Because

*Words in parentheses are omitted from some Greek manuscripts.

God raises the dead and gives them life, so also the Child of God gives life to people by choice. [22]God judges no one, but has given all judging to the Child, [23]that all may honor the Child, even as they honor the parent. Anyone who does not honor a child, does dishonor to the parent from whom the child proceeds. [24]Thus truly I tell you, anyone who hears my word and trusts the one who sent me, has eternal life; that person does not come into judgment, but has passed out of death into life.

[25]"Thus truly I tell you, the hour is coming, and now is, when the dead will hear the voice of the Child of God, and those who hear will live. [26]For as God generates life, so it has been given the Child of God also to generate life, [27]and the Child has been given authority to execute judgment, because this one is also the Child of Humanity. [28]Do not marvel at this, for the hour is coming when all who are in the tombs will hear a voice [29]and come forth, those who have done good to the resurrection of life, and those who have done evil to the resurrection of judgment.

[30]"I can do nothing on my own authority. As I hear, I judge. And my judgment is just, because I seek not my own will but the will of the one who sent me. [31]If I witness concerning myself, my testimony is not valid. [32]There is another who witnesses concerning me, and I know that the testimony which that witness states concerning me is true. [33]You have sent to John, and he has witnessed to the truth. [34]But I do not receive the testimony from humans. I say this that you may be saved. [35]John was a burning and shining lamp, and you were willing to rejoice for a while in his light.

[36]"But I have a testimony greater than that of John; for the works which God has given me to finish, these very works which I am doing, testify that God has sent me. [37]And having sent me God witnessed concerning me. You have never heard the voice nor seen the form of God. [38]You do not have God's word living in you, since you do not believe the one whom God has sent.

[39]"You search the scriptures, because you think that in them eternal life is to be found; yet it is they that testify about me. [40]But you do not wish to come to me for life.

[41]"I do not receive glory from people, [42]but I know that you do not have the love of God in you. [43]I have come in the name of

God, and you do not receive me; if another comes in his or her own name, that one you will receive. [44]How can you believe? You that receive glory from one another and do not even look for the glory that comes from the only God?

[45]"Do not think that I shall accuse you to God; the one who accuses you is Moses, on whom you set your hope. [46]If you believed Moses, you would believe me, for he wrote of me. [47]But if you do not believe the writings of Moses, how will you believe my words?"

Chapter VI

[1]AFTER THIS Jesus went away, across the Sea of Galilee, which is the Sea of Tiberias. [2]And a large crowd followed because they saw the signs which he did on those who were sick. [3]Jesus went up the mountain, and there sat down with his disciples. [4]The Passover, the feast of the Judeans, was near.

[5]Lifting up his eyes then and seeing that a large crowd was coming to him, Jesus said to Philip, "How shall we buy bread, so that these people may eat?"

[6]Jesus said this to test Philip, for Jesus knew what he would do. [7]Philip answered him, "Two hundred denarii would not buy enough bread for each of them to get a little."

[8]One of the disciples, Andrew, Simon Peter's brother, said to Jesus, [9]"There is a boy here who has five barley loaves and two fish, but what are they among so many?"

[10]Jesus said, "Have the people sit down."

Now there was a grassy place, so the people sat down, about five thousand of them. [11]Jesus then took the loaves and having given thanks distributed them to those who were seated, so also the fish, as much as they wanted. [12]And when they were filled, Jesus told his disciples, "Gather up the fragments left over, so that nothing is lost."

[13]So they gathered them up and filled twelve baskets with fragments from the five barley loaves, left by those who had eaten. [14]When the people saw the sign that Jesus had done, they said, "This is certainly the prophet who is to come into the world!"

[15]Perceiving then that they were about to come and try to make

him king, Jesus withdrew again to the mountain, alone.

[16]When evening came, his disciples went down to the sea, [17]got into a boat, and started across the sea toward Capernaum. It was dark, and Jesus had not yet come to them. [18]The sea rose because a strong wind was blowing. [19]When they had rowed three or four miles, they saw Jesus walking on the sea, coming near the boat, and they were frightened. [20]But he said to them, "It is I; do not be afraid."

[21]They were glad to take him into the boat, and immediately the boat was at the land to which they were going.

[22]On the next day the crowd standing on the other side of the sea saw that only one boat had gone, and that Jesus had not gone with his disciples, but that his disciples had gone away alone. [23]Other boats from Tiberias came near the place where they ate the bread after Jesus had given thanks. [24]So when the crowd saw that Jesus was not there, nor his disciples, they got into the boats and went to Capernaum, seeking Jesus.

[25]When they found him on the other side of the sea, they said to him, "Rabbi, when did you come here?"

[26]Jesus answered them, "Thus truly I tell you, you seek me, not because you saw signs, but because you ate the bread and were satisfied. [27]Do not work for food that perishes, but for the food which endures to eternal life, which Humanity's Child will give to you; for to this God, who is the source of my being, has attested."

[28]Then they said to him, "What shall we do to work the works of God?"

[29]Jesus answered them, "This is the work of God, that you believe in the one whom God has sent."

[30]So they said to him, "Then what sign do you do, that we may see and believe you? What work? [31]Our ancestors ate the manna in the desert; as it is written, 'They were given bread from heaven to eat.'" *(Neh 9.15)*

[32]Jesus then said to them, "Thus truly I tell you, it was not Moses who gave you the bread from heaven, but God gives you the true bread from heaven. [33]For the bread of God is the one who comes from heaven, and gives life to the world."

[34]They said to him, "Sir, give us this bread always."

[35]Jesus said to them, "I am the bread of life; anyone who comes to me shall not hunger, and anyone who believes in me shall never thirst. [36]But I told you that though you have seen me, you do not believe. [37]All those whom God gives me will come to me, and those who come to me I will not throw out. [38]For I have come from heaven, not to do my own will, but to do the will of the one who sent me. [39]And this is the will of the one who sent me, that I shall not lose anything of all that has been given me, but raise it up on the last day. [40]For this is the will of God, that everyone who sees and believes in the Child of God may have eternal life, and I will raise the believer up on the last day."

[41]The Judeans then murmured at him, because he said "I am the bread which came from heaven."

[42]They said, "Is not this Jesus, the child of Mary and Joseph, whose father and mother we know? How does he now say, 'I have come from heaven'?"

[43]Jesus answered them, "Do not murmur among yourselves. [44]No one can come to me unless God who sent me attracts that person. And I will raise up each one on the last day. [45]It is written in the prophets, 'And they shall all be taught by God.' *(Is 54.13)* Everyone who has heard and learned from God comes to me. [46]Not that anyone has seen God except the one who is from God; this one has seen God. [47]Thus truly I tell you, any one who believes has eternal life.

[48]"I am the bread of life. [49]Your ancestors ate the manna in the desert and they died. [50]This is the bread which comes out of heaven, and anyone may eat it and not die. [51]I am the living bread which came out of heaven; and the bread which I shall give, my flesh, is for the life of the world."

[52]The Judeans then argued among themselves, saying, "How can this man give us his flesh to eat?"

[53]So Jesus said to them, "Thus truly I tell you, unless you eat the flesh and drink the blood of Humanity's Child, you have no life in you. [54]All who eat my flesh and drink my blood have eternal life, and I will raise them up at the last day. [55]For my flesh is food indeed, and my blood is drink indeed. [56]All who eat my flesh and drink my blood abide in me, and I in them. [57]As God has sent me,

and I live because of God, so anyone who eats me will live because of me. [58]This is the bread which came from heaven, not such as the ancestors ate and died. Whoever eats this bread will live forever." [59]Jesus said this in the Synagogue as he taught at Capernaum.

[60]Many of his disciples, when they heard it, said, "This is a hard saying. Who can bear it?"

[61]But Jesus, knowing in himself that his disciples murmured at it, said to them, "This offends you? [62]Then what if you were to see Humanity's Child ascending where I was in the beginning? [63]It is the spirit that gives life, the flesh profits nothing; the words that I have spoken to you are spirit and life. [64]But there are some of you that do not believe." For Jesus knew from the first who those were that did not believe, and who it was that would betray him. [65]And he said, "This is why I told you that no one can come to me unless it has been given to her or him from God."

[66]After this many of his disciples drew back and no longer walked about with him. [67]Jesus said to the twelve, "Do you also wish to go away?"

[68]Simon Peter answered him, "Sir, to whom shall we go? You have the words of eternal life; [69]we believe, and we know that you are the Holy One of God."

[70]Jesus answered them, "Did I not choose you, the twelve, and one of you is a devil?" [71]Jesus spoke of Judas the son of Simon Iscariot, for Judas, one of the twelve, was going to betray Jesus.

Chapter VII

[1]AFTER THIS Jesus went about in Galilee, not in Judea, because the Judeans were seeking to kill him. [2]Now the Judean feast of Tabernacles was near. [3]So his brothers said to Jesus, "You should leave here and go to Judea, that your disciples may see the works you are doing. [4]For no one does things secretly if seeking to be known openly. If you do these things, show yourself to the world." [5]His brothers did not believe in him.

[6]Jesus said to them, "My time has not yet come but your time is always here. [7]The world cannot hate you, but it hates me because I testify that its works are evil. [8]You go to the feast; I am not going

up to this feast, for my time has not come." [9]After saying these things to them, Jesus remained in Galilee.

[10]But when his brothers had gone to the feast, then Jesus also went, not publicly, but in secret. [11]The Judeans looked for him at the feast, and said, "Where is that man?"

[12]There was much murmuring about Jesus among the crowds. Some said, "He is a good person."

Others said, "No, he deceives people."

[13]No one, however, spoke openly about Jesus, because of fear of the Judeans.

[14]But midway through the feast Jesus went up into the temple and taught. [15]The Judeans marveled and said, "How can this Jesus have knowledge without having studied?"

[16]So Jesus answered them and said, "My teaching is not mine, but is from the one who sent me. [17]Any one who wants to do the will of God will recognize whether this teaching is from God or whether I speak only from myself. [18]People who speak from themselves seek their own glory, but because I seek the glory of the one who sent me, I am true, and in me there is no falsehood. [19]Did not Moses give you the law? And not one of you keeps the law. Why is it me you seek to kill?"

[20]The crowd answered, "You have a demon! Who seeks to kill you?"

[21]Jesus answered them, saying, "I did one thing, and all of you marvel. [22]Consider this. Moses gave you circumcision (not that it is from Moses, but from the ancestors), and you circumcise a male upon the sabbath. [23]If one can receive circumcision on the sabbath so as not to break the law of Moses, why are you angry with me for making a whole person healthy on the sabbath? [24]Do not judge by appearance alone, but judge with sound judgment."

[25]Then some of the Jerusalemites said, "Is not this the man whom they seek to kill? [26]But here he is, speaking openly, and they say nothing to him! Do you suppose the authorities know in fact that this is the Christ? [27]Yet we know where this person comes from, and when the Christ appears, no one will know from where."

[28]Then Jesus shouted as he taught in the temple, "You know

me, and you know where I come from! And I have not come from myself, but that one is true who sent me, and that one you do not know. 29I know and proceed from God, the one who sent me.''

30They sought, therefore, to arrest Jesus, but no one seized him, because the time was not yet come. 31Many in the crowd believed Jesus, and said, "When the Christ appears, will more signs be done than this person has done?''

32The Pharisees heard the crowd thus murmuring about Jesus, and the chief priests and Pharisees sent their attendants to make the arrest. 33Jesus said, "For a little time I remain with you, and then I return to the one who sent me. 34You will seek me and you will not find me, and where I am you cannot come.''

35The Judeans said to one another, "Where is this man going that we will not find him? Does he expect to go to the dispersion among the Greeks and teach the Greeks? 36What is this thing he said, 'You will seek me and you will not find,' and 'Where I am you cannot come'?''

37On the last day of the feast, the great day, Jesus stood up and shouted, "If anyone thirst, come to me and drink. 38If you believe in me, as the scripture has said, 'Out of your belly shall flow rivers of living water.''' 39Now this he said about the spirit, whom those who believed were soon to receive; for at that time the spirit had not been given, because Jesus was not yet glorified.

40Hearing these words, some in the crowd said, "This is truly the prophet.''

41Others said, "This is the Christ.''

But some said, "Is the Christ to come from Galilee? 42Does not the scripture say that the Christ is a descendant of David and Bathsheba, and comes from Bethlehem, the village where David grew up?''

43So there was a division in the crowd about Jesus. 44Some of them wanted to arrest him, but no one laid hands on him.

45The attendants went back to the chief priests and Pharisees, who said to them, "Why did you not bring him?''

46The attendants answered, "No one ever spoke as this man speaks.''

47The Pharisees answered them, "Have you also been deceived? [48]Have any of the rulers or of the Pharisees believed in this man? [49]But this crowd, not knowing the law, is cursed."

[50]Nicodemus, who had earlier gone to Jesus, and who was one of the rulers, said to them, [51]"Does our law judge a person without first giving a hearing and learning what the person is doing?"

[52]The others replied, "Are you from Galilee too? Search and see that no prophet is to come out of Galilee."

They went then to their own houses.

Chapter VIII

[1]BUT JESUS WENT to the Mount of Olives.

[2]At dawn he arrived again at the temple; all the people came to Jesus, and he sat down and taught them.

[3]The scribes and Pharisees led in a woman who had been caught in adultery, and standing her in their midst, [4]they said, "Teacher, this woman has been caught in the act of adultery. [5]Now in the law, Moses commanded us to stone such. What do you say?" [6]They said this to tempt Jesus, in order to have something of which to accuse him.

Jesus stooped down and wrote on the ground with his finger. [7]But as they continued to question him, Jesus stood up and said to them, "Let the one who is without sin among you be the first to throw a stone at her."

[8]Again he bent down and wrote on the ground with his finger. [9]When they heard it, they went out one by one, beginning with the older ones, and Jesus was left alone with the woman standing there. [10]Jesus stood up and said to her, "Woman, where are they? Has no one condemned you?"

[11]She said, "No one, Sir."

Jesus said, "Neither do I condemn you; go and do not sin any more."*

[12]Again Jesus spoke to the Judeans, saying, "I am the light of the world; anyone who follows me will never walk in darkness, but will have the light of life."

[13]The Pharisees then said to him, "You are witnessing concerning yourself; your testimony is not valid."

---

*Although no one seems to doubt the authenticity of this incident, many scholars believe it misplaced here.

[14]Jesus answered, "Even if I do witness about myself, my testimony is true, because I know where I have come from and where I am going, but you do not know where I come from or where I am going. [15]You judge according to the flesh; I judge no one. [16]Yet even if I do judge, my judgment is true, for it is not I alone that judge, but I and the one who sent me. [17]Even in your law it is written that the testimony of two persons is true. [18]I am witnessing to myself, and the one who sent me also witnesses concerning me."

[19]They said to Jesus, therefore, "Where is the one who sent you?"

Jesus answered, "You know neither me nor the one who sent me; if you knew me, you would know my source also." [20]These words he spoke in the treasury as he taught in the temple but no one seized him because the time had not yet come.

[21]Again Jesus said to them, "I am going away, and you will seek me and die in your sin. Where I am going, you cannot come."

[22]Then the Judeans said, "Will he kill himself, since he says, 'Where I am going, you cannot come'?"

[23]Jesus said to them, "You are from below, I am from above. You are of this world, I am not of this world. [24]I told you that you would die in your sins, for you will die in your sins unless you believe what I am."

[25]The Judeans said to Jesus, "Who are you?"

Jesus replied, "Why do I speak to you at all! [26]I have much to say about you and much to judge, but the one who sent me is true, and I declare to the world what I have heard from that one."

[27]They did not understand that he spoke to them of God. [28]So Jesus said, "When you lift up the Child of Humanity, then you will know what I am, and that I do nothing on my own, but say things as taught by the one who sent me. [29]And the one who sent me remains with me, and has never left me alone, for I always do what is pleasing to that one."

[30]As Jesus said these things, many believed. [31]He then said to the Judeans who believed him, "If you continue in my word, you are truly my disciples, [32]and you will know the truth, and the truth will free you."

[33]They answered him, "We are descendants of Abraham and

Sarah, and have never been enslaved to anyone. How is it that you say, 'You will become free'?"

[34]Jesus answered them, "Thus truly I tell you, everyone who commits sin is a slave of sin. [35]The slave does not continue in the house forever; the heir continues forever. [36]So if the heir frees you, you will be really free. [37]I know that you are descendants of Sarah and Abraham, but you seek to kill me, because my word finds no place in you. [38]I speak of what I have seen with my parent, and you do what you have heard from your parents."

[39]They answered him, "Abraham and Sarah are our parents."

Jesus said to them, "If you were Sarah and Abraham's children, you would do what they did. [40]But now you seek to kill me, a person who has told you the truth which I heard from God; this is not what Sarah and Abraham did. [41]But you do what your parents did."

They said to him, "We were not born of fornication; we have one parentage, even God."

[42]Jesus said to them, "If God were your parent, you would love me, for I proceeded and came forth from God, not from myself. God sent me. [43]Why do you not understand what I say? Because you cannot hear my word. [44]Your parentage is from the devil and your will is to do that parent's desires. That one was a murderer from the beginning, and did not stand in truth, because there is no truth in the devil. When lying, the devil speaks out of its own nature, for the devil is a liar and the source of all lies. [45]Because I tell the truth, you do not believe me.[46]Who among you accuses me of sin? If I tell the truth, why do you not believe me? [47]Anyone who belongs to God is able to hear the words of God. The reason why you cannot hear is because you do not belong to God."

[48]The Judeans responded, "Are we not right in saying that you are a Samaritan and have a demon?"

[49]Jesus answered, "I do not have a demon. I honor my parentage, and you dishonor me. [50]I do not seek my own glory, but there is one who seeks my glory and is the judge of all. [51]Thus truly I tell you, anyone who keeps my word will never see death."

[52]The Judeans said to him, "Now we know that you have a de-

mon. Abraham and Sarah died, also the prophets, but you say, 'Anyone who keeps my word will never taste death.' ⁵³Are you greater than our ancestors Sarah and Abraham, who died? And the prophets died! Who do you think you are?"

⁵⁴Jesus answered, "If I glorify myself, my glory is nothing; the one who sent me is the one who glorifies me, of whom you say that this is our God. ⁵⁵You have not known God, but I do. If I say, 'I do not know God,' I would be a liar like you; but I do know God and I keep God's word. ⁵⁶Your ancestor Abraham was glad that he would see my day; he saw it and rejoiced.

⁵⁷The Judeans then said to him, "You are not yet fifty years old, and have you seen Abraham?"

⁵⁸Jesus said to them, "Thus truly I tell you, before Abraham was, I am."

⁵⁹So they picked up stones to throw at him, but Jesus was hidden, and went out of the temple.

Chapter IX

¹PASSING BY, Jesus saw a man blind from birth. ²And his disciples asked, "Rabbi, who sinned, this man or his parents, that he was born blind?"

³Jesus answered, "Neither this man nor his parents sinned, but his blindness allows that the works of God might be made manifest in him. ⁴We must work the works of God while it is day; night comes, when no one can work. ⁵While I am in the world, I am the light of the world."

⁶Having said this, Jesus spat on the ground, made clay of the spittle and put the clay on the man's eyes, ⁷then said to him, "Go, wash in the pool of Siloam" (which means sent). So the man went and washed and came back seeing.

⁸The neighbors and those who had seen him before as a beggar said, "Is this not the man who used to sit and beg?"

⁹Some said, "This is he."

Others said, "No, but he is like him."

The man said, "I am the one."

¹⁰So they asked, "Then how were your eyes opened?"

11He answered, "The man named Jesus made clay and anointed my eyes and told me to go to Siloam and wash; so I went, and washed, and saw."

12They said to the one who had been blind, "Where is this Jesus?"

He replied, "I do not know."

13The neighbors led the one who had been blind to the Pharisees. 14It was a sabbath day when Jesus made the clay and opened the blind eyes. 15Now the Pharisees asked the man how he had received his sight. And the one who had been blind said to them, "Jesus put clay on my eyes, and I washed, and I see."

16Some of the Pharisees said, "This Jesus can not be from God, for he does not keep the sabbath."

But others said, "How could a sinful person do such signs?"

There was a division among them. 17So they again said to the one who had been blind, "What do you say about Jesus, since your eyes have been opened?"

He replied, "Jesus is a prophet."

18The Judeans did not believe that the man had been blind and now saw, until they called the parents of the one who had received sight, 19and asked them, "Is this your son, who you say was born blind? How then does he now see?"

20The parents answered, "We know that this is our son, and that he was born blind. 21But how he now sees we do not know, nor do we know who opened his eyes. Ask him; he is of age and will speak for himself."

22The parents said these things because they feared the Judeans, for the Judeans had already agreed that anyone who acknowledged Jesus to be the Christ, would be put out of the synagogue. 23Therefore the parents said, "He is of age, ask him."

24So a second time they called the one who had been blind and said to him, "Give glory to God. We know that this Jesus is sinful."

25The man answered, "If sinful or not, I do not know. One thing I know: I was blind, now I see."

26The Pharisees said, "What did he do to you? How did he open your eyes?"

27The one born blind answered them, "I have told you already, and you did not hear me. Why do you want to hear it again? Do you also want to become his disciples?"

28They reviled him, saying, "You are a disciple of Jesus, but we are disciples of Moses. 29We know that God spoke through Moses, but this one, we do not know where he is from."

30The man answered them, "Why this is a marvelous thing! You do not know where Jesus is from, and he opened my eyes. 31We know that God does not listen to sinners, but if anyone is a worshiper of God and does God's will, God listens to that person. 32Not since the world began has it been heard that anyone opened the eyes of a person born blind. 33If Jesus were not from God, he could not do anything."

34The Pharisees answered, "You were born in total sin, and you would teach us!" And they threw him out.

35Jesus heard that they had thrown out the one born blind, and finding him said, "Do you believe in the Child of Humanity?"

36The man answered, "And who is this Child of Humanity, sir, that I might believe?"

37Jesus said, "You have seen and I who speak to you am that one."

38He answered, "I believe, sir," and worshiped Jesus.

39Jesus said, "For judgment I came into this world, that those not able to see may see, and those who see become blind."

40Some of the Pharisees who were with them heard this, and said to Jesus, "We are not blind, are we?"

41Jesus said to them, "If you were blind, you would have no sin; but now that you say, 'We see,' your sin persists."

Chapter X

1"THUS TRULY I tell you, the one who does not enter the sheepfold by the door, but climbs in by another way, is a thief and a robber, 2but the one who enters by the door is the shepherd of the sheep. 3To this one the doorkeeper opens, the sheep hear the shepherd's voice, and the sheep are called, each by name, and led out by their own shepherd. 4Having brought out the sheep of the flock, the shepherd goes before them, and the sheep follow for they know their shepherd's voice. [5]They will not follow a stranger, but will flee from strangers for they do not know their voices."

[6]Jesus used this metaphor with them, but they did not understand what he was talking about.

[7]So Jesus again said to them, "Thus truly I tell you, I am the door of the sheep. [8]All who came before me were thieves and robbers, but the sheep did not hear them. [9]I am the door; anyone who enters through me will be saved, and will go in and will go out and will find pasture. [10]The thief comes only to steal and kill and destroy. I came that they may have life, and have it with abundance. [11]I am the good shepherd. The good shepherd would die for the sheep. [12]The hireling, who is not the shepherd, whose own the sheep are not, sees the wolf coming, leaves the sheep, and runs away; the wolf seizes them and scatters them. [13]The hireling cares nothing for the sheep. [14]I am the good shepherd; I know my own and my own know me, [15]as the one to whom I belong knows me and I know that one. I lay down my life for my sheep, [16]and I have other sheep, that are not of this fold. I must gather them also, and they will hear my voice; then there will be one flock and one shepherd. [17]For this reason God loves me, because I lay down my life, that I may take it again. [18]No one takes it from me but I myself lay it down. I have authority to lay it down, and I have authority to take it again; this commandment I received from God."

[19]Again there was a division among the Judeans because of these words. [20]Many of them said, "He has a demon, and he raves; why listen to him?"

[21]Others said, "These are not the words of one who is demon-possessed. Can a demon open the eyes of the blind?"

[22]There was then the Feast of the Dedication at Jerusalem. It was winter, [23]and Jesus walked in the temple, in the porch of Solomon. [24]The Judeans surrounded him and said, "How long will you hold us in suspense? If you are the Christ, tell us plainly."

[25]Jesus answered them, "I told you, and you do not believe. The works that I do in the name of God witness to me, [26]but you do not believe, because you are not my sheep. [27]My sheep hear my voice; I know them and they follow me. [28]I give them eternal life

and they shall not perish; no one shall seize them from my hand. [29]The one who sent me is greater than all, and has given the sheep to me. No one can seize what is in God's possession. [30]I and God who sent me are one."

[31]The Judeans took up stones again to stone him. [32]Jesus answered them, "I have shown you many good works from God. For which of these works do you stone me?"

[33]The Judeans answered him, "We do not stone you for a good work, but for blasphemy; because you, being human, make yourself God."

[34]Jesus answered them, "Is it not written in your law, 'I said, you are gods'? [35]If the person to whom the word of God came called them gods (and scripture cannot be broken), [36]do you say to the one whom God sanctified and sent into the world, 'You are blaspheming,' because I said, 'I am the child of God'? [37]If I do not do the works of God, then do not believe me; [38]but if I do them, even though you do not believe me, believe the works, that you may know and understand that God is in me and I am in God."

[39]Again they tried to arrest Jesus, but he escaped from their hands.

[40]Jesus went away again across the Jordan to the place where John at first had been baptizing, and he stayed there. [41]Many came to Jesus and said, "John did no sign, but everything that John said about this man was true." [42]And many in that place believed in Jesus.

Chapter XI

[1]NOW A CERTAIN MAN was sick, Lazarus of Bethany the village of Mary and her sister Martha. [2]Mary was the one who anointed Jesus with ointment and wiped his feet with her hair; her brother Lazarus was sick. [3]So the sisters sent word to Jesus, saying, "Sir, one whom you love is sick."

[4]Hearing this, Jesus said, "This sickness is not to end in death, but is for the glory of God, so that the Child of God may be glorified through it."

[5]Now Jesus loved Martha and Mary and Lazarus. [6]But having

heard that Lazarus was sick, Jesus still remained two more days in the place where he was. [7]Then after this Jesus said to the disciples, "Let us go to Judea again."

[8]The disciples said to him, "Rabbi, the Judeans were just now seeking to stone you. Are you going there again?"

[9]Jesus answered, "Are there not twelve hours in the day? Anyone walking the daylight does not stumble, because the light of this world is present. [10]But anyone walking in the night stumbles because the light is not there."

[11]After saying these things, he then said to them, "Our friend Lazarus has fallen asleep, but I am going to awaken him."

[12]The disciples said, "Sir, if Lazarus has fallen asleep, he will recover."

[13]Now Jesus had spoken of Lazarus's death, but they thought that he meant restful slumber. [14]Then Jesus told them plainly, "Lazarus died. [15]I rejoice for you that I was not there, so that you may believe. Let us go to him."

[16]Thomas, called the Twin, said to the other disciples, "Let us also go, that we may die with Jesus."

[17]When Jesus arrived, he found that Lazarus had already been in the tomb for four days. [18]Bethany was near Jerusalem, about two miles away, [19]and many of the Judeans had come to Martha and Mary to console them concerning their brother. [20]When Martha heard that Jesus was coming, she went to meet him, while Mary sat in the house. [21]Martha said to Jesus, "Sir, if you had been here, my brother would not have died. [22]Even now I know that whatever you ask from God, God will give you."

[23]Jesus said to her, "Your brother will rise again."

[24]Martha said to him, "I know that Lazarus will rise again in the resurrection on the last day."

[25]Jesus said to her, "I am the resurrection and the life; all those who believe in me, even if they die, they will live. [26]And all who live and believe in me will never die. Do you believe this?"

[27]She said to him, "Yes, Sir, I believe that you are the Christ, the Child of God, the One coming into the world."

[28]When she had said this, Martha went and called her sister Mary, saying secretly, "The Teacher is here and is calling for you."

²⁹When Mary heard it, she rose quickly and went to Jesus. ³⁰Now Jesus had not yet come to the village, but was still at the place where Martha had met him. ³¹The Judeans who were with Mary in the house, consoling her, saw Mary rise quickly and go out, and they followed, thinking that she was going to the tomb to weep there.

³²When Mary came where Jesus was and saw him, she fell at his feet, saying to him, "Sir, if you had been here, my brother would not have died."

³³When Jesus saw her weeping, and the Judeans who came with her also weeping, he groaned in spirit and was troubled. ³⁴And he said, "Where have you put him?"

They answered, "Sir, come and see."

³⁵Jesus wept.

³⁶The Judeans said, "See how he loved Lazarus!"

³⁷But some of them said, "Could not this Jesus who opened the eyes of the blind have prevented Lazarus from dying?"

³⁸Then Jesus, again groaning within, came to the tomb which was a cave with a stone lying on it. ³⁹Jesus said, "Lift away the stone."

Martha, the sister of the dead man, said to Jesus, "Sir, by now there will be a bad odor, for it is the fourth day."

⁴⁰Jesus said to her, "Did I not tell you that if you believe you will see the glory of God?"

⁴¹So they lifted the stone. And Jesus lifted up his eyes and spoke, "God, I thank you that you have heard me. ⁴²I know that you always hear me, but I have said this so that the crowd standing here may believe that you did send me."

⁴³After saying this, Jesus shouted with a loud voice, "Lazarus, come out."

⁴⁴The one who was dead came out, hands and feet bound with bandages, and face wrapped with a cloth. Jesus said to them, "Release Lazarus, and let him go."

⁴⁵Many of the Judeans, who had come with Mary and had seen what happened, believed in Jesus. ⁴⁶But some went to the Pharisees and told them what Jesus had done. ⁴⁷So the chief priests and the Pharisees gathered the council, and said, "What shall we do?

This Jesus performs many signs. [48]If we allow this, everyone will believe in him, and the Romans will come and take from us both the holy place and the nation."

[49]But one of them, Caiaphas, who was high priest that year, said to them, "You know nothing at all, [50]nor understand that it is expedient for us that one person should die for the people, so that the whole nation will not perish."

[51]He did not say this from himself, but being high priest that year Caiaphas prophesied that Jesus was about to die for the nation, [52]and not for the nation only, but also that the children of God who are scattered abroad might be gathered into one people. [53]From that day, they conspired to kill Jesus.

[54]Jesus therefore no longer openly walked among the Judeans but went away to the country near the desert, to a city called Ephraim, and there remained with the disciples.

[55]Now the Passover of the Judeans was near, and many went up from the country to Jerusalem before the Passover, to purify themselves. [56]They looked for Jesus and said to one another as they stood in the temple, "What do you think? That he will not come to the feast?"

[57]Now the chief priests and the Pharisees had commanded that anyone knowing where Jesus was should inform them, so that they might arrest him.

Chapter XII

[1]SIX DAYS BEFORE THE PASSOVER, Jesus came to Bethany, where Lazarus, whom Jesus had raised from the dead, lived. [2]There they made Jesus a supper. Martha served, but Lazarus was one of those reclining at the table with Jesus. [3]Mary, taking a pound of pure nard, a costly ointment, anointed the feet of Jesus and wiped his feet with her hair, and the house was filled with the fragrance of the ointment. [4]But Judas Iscariot, one of the disciples (the one who was about to betray Jesus), said, [5]"Why was this ointment not sold for three hundred denarii and the money given to the poor?"

[6]Judas said this, not because he cared about the poor, but be-

cause he was a thief, and kept the collection bag.

[7] Jesus said, "Let her alone, so that she may keep it for the day of my burial. [8] For you always have poor people with you, but you do not always have me."

[9] A great crowd of the Judeans learned that Jesus was there, and they came, not only because of Jesus but also to see Lazarus, who had been raised from the dead. [10] The chief priests made plans to kill Lazarus also, [11] for because of him many of the Judeans went along and believed in Jesus.

[12] The next day the great crowd coming to the feast heard that Jesus was coming to Jerusalem. [13] They took branches of palm trees and went out to meet him, and shouted, "Hosanna! Blessed be the one coming in the name of God, even the Leader of Israel!" *(Ps 118:25-27)*

[14] And Jesus found a young donkey and sat upon it, as it is written, [15] "Do not be afraid, child of Zion. Look, your leader is coming, sitting on the foal of a donkey!" *(Zech 9:9)*

[16] The disciples did not at first understand what was happening, but when Jesus was glorified, they remembered that these things had been written of the Christ and that the people had done these things to Jesus.

[17] The crowd that had been present when Jesus called Lazarus out of the tomb and raised him from the dead witnessed to that event. [18] And a larger crowd went to meet Jesus because they heard that he had done this sign. [19] The Pharisees then said among themselves, "You see that you gain nothing; look how the world is gone after him."

[20] Now there were Greeks among those who went up to worship at the feast. [21] So these approached Philip, who was from Bethsaida in Galilee, and requested of him, "Sir, we wish to see Jesus."

[22] Philip went and told Andrew; then Andrew and Philip went to tell Jesus. [23] And Jesus answered them, "The time has come when Humanity's Child is glorified. [24] Thus truly I tell you, unless the grain of wheat, falling into the ground, dies, it alone remains. But if it dies, it bears much fruit. [25] If you love your own life you lose it, but if you hate your own life in this world you will keep it in

eternal existence. [26]Anyone who serves me, must follow me, so that where I am, there will my servant be also. If anyone serves me, God will honor that one.

[27]"Now my soul is troubled. And what shall I say, 'God, save me from this hour'? But for this purpose I have come to this hour. [28]God, glorify your name."

Then a voice came from heaven, "I have glorified it, and I will glorify it again."

[29]The crowd standing by heard it and said that it had thundered. Others said, "An angel has spoken to him."

[30]Jesus answered, "This voice has come not for my sake, but for yours. [31]Now is the judgment of this world, now the ruler of this world will be thrown out, [32]and I, if I am lifted up from earth, will draw all people to my self."

[33]Jesus said this to show by what kind of death he would die.

[34]The crowd answered him, "We have heard from the law that the Christ remains forever. How can you say that it is necessary for the Child of Humanity to be lifted up? Who is this Child of Humanity?"

[35]Jesus said to them, "The light is with you for a little longer. Walk while you have the light, before the darkness overtakes you; when you walk in the darkness you do not know where you are going. [36]While you have the light, trust in the light, that you may become children of light."

Having said these things, Jesus departed and was hidden from them. [37]Although Jesus had done many signs before them, people did not believe in him, [38]that the word of the prophet Isaiah might be fulfilled, which said *(53:1)*, "O God, who has believed our report, and to whom was the arm of God revealed?" [39]Therefore, they could not believe, for Isaiah also said, *(6:10)* [40]"God has blinded their eyes and hardened their hearts, that they might not see with their eyes nor understand with their hearts, nor turn and I would heal them."

[41]Isaiah said this because he saw and spoke of the glory of the Christ. [42]Nevertheless even among the rulers many believed in Jesus, but because of the Pharisees they did not confess it, lest they should be put out of the synagogue, [43]for they loved the glory

given by people more than the glory of God.

[44]But Jesus shouted and said, "Anyone who believes in me, believes not in me but in the one who sent me. [45]Anyone who sees me sees the one who sent me. [46]I have come as light into the world, that everyone believing in me may not remain in darkness. [47]If anyone hears my words and does not keep them, I do not judge that one; for I came not to judge the world but that I might save the world. [48]Anyone rejecting me and not receiving my words has a judge; the word that I have spoken will judge that person on the last day. [49]For I have not spoken from myself, but the one who sent me has given me commandment what I may say and what I may speak. [50]And I know that commandment is eternal life. What I tell, therefore, I tell as God has told me."

Chapter XIII

[1]NOW BEFORE THE FEAST of the Passover, when Jesus knew that his time had come to depart from this world and go to God, and loving his own in the world, Jesus loved them to the end.

[2]During supper, after the devil had already put it into the heart of Judas the son of Simon Iscariot to betray Jesus; [3]Jesus, knowing that God had given all things into his hands and that he had come forth from God and was going to God, [4]got up from the supper, laid aside his garments, and girded himself with a towel. [5]Then Jesus put water into the basin, and began to wash the feet of the disciples, and to wipe them with the towel with which he was girded.

[6]Jesus came to Simon Peter, and Peter said to him, "Sir, do you wash my feet?"

[7]Jesus answered, "You do not yet know what I am doing, but later you will understand."

[8]Peter said to him, "You shall never wash my feet."

Jesus answered, "Unless I wash you, you have no part in me."

[9]Simon Peter said to Jesus, "Sir, not only my feet but also my hands and my head!"

[10]Jesus said to Peter, "One who has bathed has no need to wash, except for the feet, but is wholly clean; and you are clean, but not every one of you." ([11]For Jesus knew who would betray

31

him; that was why he said, "You are not all clean.")

[12]After Jesus had washed their feet, had again taken his garments, and reclined at the table, he said to them, "Do you know what I have done to you? [13]You call me the teacher, and the leader, and you are right, for I am. [14]If I then, your leader and teacher, have washed your feet, you also ought to wash one another's feet. [15]For I have given you an example, that you also may do as I have done to you. [16]Thus truly I tell you, the slave is not greater than the slave's owner, nor is one sent greater than the sender. [17]If you know these things, blessed are you if you do them. [18]I am not speaking of you all. I know whom I have chosen. But so that the scripture may be fulfilled, 'One who ate my bread turned against me.' *(Ps 41:9)* [19]I tell you this now, before it happens, so that when it happens you may know who I am. [20]Thus truly I tell you, any one who receives whomever I send receives me, and anyone receiving me receives the one who sent me."

[21]Having said these things, Jesus was troubled in spirit, and testified, "Thus truly I tell you, one of you will betray me."

[22]The disciples looked at one another and were perplexed about whom he was speaking. [23]One of them, a disciple whom Jesus loved, was reclining in the bosom of Jesus; [24]so Simon Peter nodded to that one and said, "Tell us who it is about whom he speaks."

[25]Leaning back thus on the breast of Jesus, the disciple said to him, "Sir, who is it?"

[26]Jesus answered, "It is the one to whom I shall give this morsel when I have dipped it."

Dipping the morsel, Jesus gave it to Judas, the son of Simon Iscariot. [27]After the morsel, Satan entered into Judas. Then Jesus said to him, "What you are going to do, do quickly."

[28]Now no one reclining at the table knew why Jesus said this to Judas. [29]Some thought that, because Judas had the money bag, Jesus was telling him to buy what was needed for the feast, or that he should give something to the poor. [30]So, after receiving the morsel, Judas went out immediately, and it was night.

[31]After Judas went out, Jesus said, "Now is the Child of Humanity glorified, and God is glorified in this Child. [32]If God is

glorified in the Child of Humanity, God will also glorify the Child in God, and will do so immediately.

33"Little children, for a short while I can be with you. You will seek me, and as I said to the Judeans so now I say to you, 'Where I go you cannot come.' 34A new commandment I give you, that you love one another, as I have loved you, that you also love one another. 35By this all people will know that you are my disciples, if you have love for one another."

36Simon Peter said to him, "Sir, where are you going?"

Jesus answered, "I am going where you cannot now follow me, but you will follow later."

37Peter said to him, "Sir, why can I not follow you now? I will lay down my life for you."

38Jesus answered, "Will you lay down your life for me? Thus truly I tell you, before a cock crows, you will deny me three times."

Chapter XIV

1"LET NOT YOUR HEARTS be troubled; believe in God, believe also in me. 2In the house of God are many living spaces; if it were otherwise I would have told you, because I go to prepare a place for you. 3If I go and prepare a place for you, I will come again and will receive you to myself, that where I am you also may be. 4And where I go, you know the way."

5Thomas said to him, "Sir, we do not know where you are going; how do we know the way?"

6Jesus said to him, "I am the way, and the truth, and the life; no one comes to God except through me. 7If you had known me, you would also have known the one who sent me; henceforth you know and have seen God."

8Philip said to him, "Sir, show us the one who sent you, and we shall be satisfied."

9Jesus said to him, "Have I been with you so long, and you still do not know me, Philip? Anyone who has seen me has seen the one who sent me; how can you say, 'Show us that one'? 10Do you not believe that I am in God and God is in me? The words that I say to you are not spoken from myself. God who lives in me does the work of God. [11]Believe me that I am in God and God is in me. Or, just believe because of the works.

[12]"Thus truly I tell you, all who believe in me will also do the works that I do, and greater works than these will they do, because I return to the one who sent me. [13]And whatever you ask in my name, this I will do, that God may be glorified in me. [14]If you ask anything of me in my name, I will do it.

[15]"If you love me, you will keep my commandments. [16]And I will request it, and God will give you another Counselor to be with you forever, [17]the Spirit of truth, which the world cannot receive, because the world neither sees nor knows the Spirit. You know it because it remains with you and will be in you.

[18]"I will not leave you orphans, for I am coming to you. [19]Yet a little while, and the world will see me no longer, but you see me, and because I live, you will live also. [20]On that day you will know that I am in God, and you in me, and I in you. [21]Anyone who has my commandments and keeps them, is one who loves me; and anyone who loves me, God loves. And I will love those who love me and I will manifest myself to them."

[22]Judas (not Iscariot) said to Jesus, "Sir, what has happened that you are going to manifest yourself to us, and not to the world?"

[23]Jesus answered him, "If you love me, you will keep my word, and God will love you and we will come to you and make our home with you. [24]Anyone who does not love me does not keep my words, and the word which you hear is not mine but from God who sent me.

[25]"I have told you these things while I am with you. [26]But the Counselor, the Holy Spirit, which God will send in my name, will teach you all things, and remind you of all the things I have told you.

[27]"Peace I leave to you; my peace I give you; not as the world gives do I give to you. Let not your heart be troubled, neither let it be fearful. [28]You heard what I said to you, 'I go, and I come to you.' If you loved me, you would have rejoiced, because I am returning to the Source of my being, for my Source is greater than I. [29]I have told you now before it happens so that when it does

happen, you will believe it. [30]I will no longer talk much with you for the ruler of this world is coming. The ruler is nothing to me, [31]but, that the world may know that I love God, as God has commanded me, so I do.

"Get up, let us go forth."

Chapter XV

[1]"I AM the true vine, and God is my gardener, [2]who takes away every branch of mine that bears no fruit, and who prunes every branch that does bear fruit, that it may bear more fruit. [3]Now you are clean because of the word I have spoken to you. [4]Live in me; I live in you. As the branch cannot bear fruit from itself, unless it lives in the vine, neither can you, unless you live in me. [5]I am the vine; you are the branches. If you are living in me, and I in you, you bear much fruit, while apart from me you can do nothing. [6]If men and women do not live in me, they are cut off as unproductive branches and are dried, and the dry branches are gathered, thrown into the fire, and burned. [7]If you live in me, and my words live in you, ask whatever you wish and it will happen to you. [8]If you bear much fruit, God is glorified, and you are my disciples.

[9]As God has loved me, so have I loved you; live in my love. [10]If you keep my commandments, you will live in my love, just as I have kept the commandments and live in God's love. [11]I have said these things to you, that my joy may be in you, and that your joy may be full.

[12]"This is my commandment, that you love one another as I have loved you. [13]There is no greater love than this: that you lay down your life for your friends. [14]You are my friends if you do what I command you. [15]No longer do I call you slaves, for slaves do not understand what their owner is doing; but I have called you friends, because all that I have heard from God, I have made known to you. [16]You did not choose me, but I chose you and appointed you that you should go and bear fruit and that your fruit should be lasting. So whatever you ask God in my name, will be given to you. [17]These things I command you, that you love one another.

[18]"If the world hates you, you know that it has hated me before it hated you. [19]If you were of the world, the world would love its own, but because you are not of the world, but I chose you out of the world, therefore the world hates you. [20]Remember the word that I said to you, 'A slave is not greater than the slave owner.' If they persecuted me they will persecute you; if they kept my word they will keep yours also. [21]But they will do all these things to you because of who I am and because they do not know the one who sent me. [22]If I had not come and spoken to them, they would not have sin, but now they have no cover for their sin. [23]Anyone who hates me, also hates the one who sent me. [24]If I had not done among them the works which no other person did, they would not have had sin, but now they have seen and hated both me and the one who sent me. [25]It is to fulfill the word written in their law, 'They hated me freely without cause.' [26]When the Counselor comes, whom I shall send to you from God, even the Spirit of truth, which proceeds out of the same one who sent me, the Spirit will witness concerning me, [27]and you also witness, because you are with me from the beginning.

Chapter XVI

[1]"I HAVE SAID these things to you that you may not be devastated. [2]For they will put you out of the synagogues, and the time is coming when whoever kills you will think they are offering service to God. [3]And they will do these things because they have known neither God nor me. [4]But I have said these things to you that when their time comes you may remember that I told you about them.

"I did not tell you these things from the beginning, because I was with you. [5]But now I am going to the one who sent me, and not one of you asks me, 'Where are you going?' [6]Grief has filled your hearts because I have said these things to you. [7]But I tell you the truth. It is expedient for you that I go away, for if I do not go, the Counselor can not come to you, but if I go, I will send the Spirit to you. [8]And when the Spirit comes, it will censure the world about sin and about righteousness and about judgment. [9]About sin, because they do not believe in me; [10]about righteousness, because I return to the one who sent me, and you will no longer see me; [11]of judgment, because the ruler of this world has been judged.

[12]"I have many more things to tell you, but you cannot bear them now. [13]When the Spirit of truth comes, you will be guided into all truth. For the Spirit will not speak from itself, but whatever it hears it will speak, and will declare to you things to come. [14]The Spirit will glorify me, for it will receive what is mine and declare it to you. [15]All things which God has are mine; therefore, I said that the Spirit will receive what is mine and declare it to you.

[16]"A little while, and you will see me no more; again a little while, and you will see me."

[17]Some of his disciples said to one another, "What is this that Jesus tells us? 'A little while, and you will not see me, and again a little while, and you will see me.' and 'Because I return to the one who sent me.'"

[18]They said, therefore, "What is this which he says, the 'little while'? We do not know what Jesus means."

[19]Jesus, knowing that they wanted to question him, said to them, "Is this what you are asking one another, what I meant by saying, 'A little while, and you will not see me, and again a little while and you will see me'? [20]Thus truly I tell you, you will weep and lament, and the world will rejoice. You will grieve, but your grief will become joy. [21]A woman giving birth has grief, because her time has come, but when she brings forth the child, she no longer remembers the distress, because of the joy that a human being is born into the world. [22]So you have grief now, but I will see you again and your hearts will rejoice, and no one will take your joy from you. [23]In that day you will not question anything. Thus truly I tell you, whatever you ask of God will be given to you in my name. [24]Until now you asked nothing in my name. Ask, and you will receive, that your joy may be complete.

[25]"I have said this to you in metaphor. The time is coming when I shall no longer speak to you in metaphor but will tell you plainly about God. [26]In that day you will ask in my name, and I do not tell you that I shall request God for you, [27]for God directly loves you, because you have loved me and have believed that I came from God. [28]I came from the Source of my being and have come

into the world, again I am leaving the world and returning to my Source."

[29]His disciples said, "Now you are speaking plainly, not in any metaphor! [30]Now we know that you know all things, and have no need for anyone to question you; by this we believe that you came from God."

[31]Jesus answered them, "Now you believe? [32]The time is coming, has in fact come, when you are scattered, each to your own home, leaving me alone, but I am not alone, for God is with me. [33]I have said these things to you, that you may have peace in me. In the world you have distress, but be of good cheer, I have overcome the world."

Chapter XVII

[1]HAVING SPOKEN these words, Jesus lifted up his eyes to heaven and said, "My God, Source of my being, the hour has come. Glorify your child that your child may glorify you, [2]as you have given me authority over all flesh, that I may give eternal life to all whom you gave me. [3]And this is eternal life, that they may know you, the only true God, and Jesus Christ whom you have sent. [4]I glorified you on earth, and finished the work which you gave me to do. [5]And now, glorify me with you, with the glory which I had with you before the world existed.

[6]"I have manifested your name to the people whom you gave me out of the world. They were yours and you gave them to me, and they have kept your word. [7]Now they know that all things that you have given me are from you, [8]for I have given them the words which you gave me, and they have received them and know in truth that I came forth from you, and they have believed that you sent me. [9]I am making a request for them, for they are yours. [10]All mine are yours, and yours are mine, and I am glorified in them. [11]And I am no longer in the world, but they are in the world, and I come to you. Holy One, Source of my being, keep them in your name which you have given me, that they may be one just as we are one. [12]While I was with them, I kept them in your name which you have given me; I guarded them, and not one perished, except that

offspring of perdition, that the scripture might be fulfilled. [13]But now I come to you, and I speak these things in the world that they may have my joy fulfilled in themselves. [14]I have given them your word, and the world has hated them because they are not of the world, just as I am not of the world. [15]I do not request that you would take them out of the world, but that you would keep them from evil. [16]They are not of the world, just as I am not of the world. [17]Sanctify them in the truth; your word is truth. [18]As you sent me into the world, I also sent them into the world. [19]And on their behalf I sanctify myself, that they also may be sanctified in truth.

[20]"I do not plead for these only, but also for those who will believe in me through their word, [21]that they may all be one, as you are in me, and I in you, that they also may be in us, so that the world may believe that you sent me. [22]The glory which you give me I give to them, that they may be one just as we are one, [23]I in them and you in me, that they may become perfected, being one, so that the world may know that you sent me and love them just as you love me.

[24]"As to those whom you have given me, I desire that they may be with me where I am, to perceive my glory which you have given me because you loved me before the foundation of the world.

[25]"Righteous God, the world did not know you, but I knew you, and these know that you sent me. [26]I made your name known to them, and I will make it known, that the love with which you have loved me may be in them, and I in them."

Chapter XVIII

[1]HAVING SPOKEN these words, Jesus went forth with his disciples across the Kidron valley, where there was a garden, which he and his disciples entered. [2]Now Judas, the betrayer, also knew the place; for Jesus often gathered his disciples there. [3]So Judas, leading a band of attendants from the chief priests and from the Pharisees, came there with lanterns, torches, and weapons. [4]Then Jesus, knowing all that was to come, went forward and said to them, "Whom do you seek?"

[5]They answered him, "Jesus of Nazareth."

Jesus told them, "I am the one."

Judas, the betrayer, stood with them. [6]When Jesus said to them, "I am the one," they backed away and fell on the ground.

[7]Again Jesus asked them, "Whom do you seek?"

And they said, "Jesus of Nazareth."

[8]Jesus answered, "I told you that I am the one. If, therefore, you seek me, let these others go."

[9]This was to fulfil the word Jesus had spoken, "Of those whom you gave me I lost not one." *(John 17:12)*

[10]Then Simon Peter, having a sword, drew it and struck the high priest's slave and cut off his right ear. The slave's name was Malchus. [11]Jesus said to Peter, "Put the sword into its sheath; shall I not drink the cup which God has given me?"

[12]So the Judean band of attendants and their captain seized Jesus, bound him, [13]and led him first to Annas, for he was the father-in-law of Caiaphas, who was high priest that year. [14]It was Caiaphas who had advised the Judeans that it was expedient for one person to die for the people.

[15]Simon Peter and another disciple followed Jesus. This disciple was known to the high priest, and entered the court of the high priest with Jesus, [16]while Peter stood at the outside door. So the other disciple, who was known to the high priest, went out and spoke to the woman who kept the door, and brought Peter in. [17]The woman who kept the door said to Peter, "Are you not also one of this man's disciples?"

Peter said, "I am not."

[18]Now the slaves and attendants, having made a fire because it was cold, were warming themselves. Peter was also with them, standing and warming himself.

[19]The high priest then questioned Jesus about his disciples and about his teaching. [20]Jesus answered him, "I have spoken openly to the world; I always taught in synagogues and in the temple, where all Judeans came together; I have said nothing in secret. [21]Why do you question me? Ask those who have heard me, what I said. They know what I said."

[22]When he said this, one of the attendants standing by struck

Jesus, saying, "Is that how you answer the high priest?"

23 Jesus answered him, "If I have spoken evil, testify about the evil; but if I spoke correctly why do you strike me?"

24 Annas then sent Jesus bound to Caiaphas the high priest.

25 Now Simon Peter was standing and warming himself. They said to him, "Are not you also one of the disciples of Jesus?"

Peter denied it and said, "I am not."

26 One of the slaves of the high priest, a relative of the one whose ear Peter had cut off, asked, "Did I not see you in the garden with Jesus?"

27 Peter again denied it, and at once a cock crowed.

28 Then they led Jesus from Caiaphas to the praetorium. It was early. They themselves did not enter the praetorium, so that they would not be defiled, but could eat the passover. 29 Therefore, Pilate went outside to them and said, "What accusation do you bring against this man?"

30 They answered, "If this man were not doing evil, we would not have delivered him to you."

31 Pilate said to them, "Take him yourselves and judge him according to your own law."

The Judeans said to him, "It is not lawful for us to kill any one."

32 This was to fulfil the words of Jesus, that he had spoken signifying by what death he would die.

33 Pilate re-entered the praetorium and called Jesus, and said to him, "Are you the ruler of the Judeans?"

34 Jesus answered, "Do you say this from yourself, or did others tell you about me?"

35 Pilate answered, "Am I a Judean? Your own nation and the chief priests have delivered you to me. What have you done?"

36 Jesus answered, "That which I rule is not of this world. If I ruled in this world, my attendants would have fought to prevent my being delivered to the Judeans. My power is not worldly."

37 Pilate said to Jesus, "Then you have power to rule?"

Jesus answered, "You say that I have ruling power; for this I was born, and for this I have come into the world, to testify to the truth. Everyone who belongs to truth hears my voice."

38Pilate said to him, "What is truth?"

Having said this, Pilate went out to the Judeans again, and told them, "I find no crime in this man. 39But you have a custom that I should release one prisoner to you at the Passover; will you have me release to you the ruler of the Judeans?"

40They cried out again, "Not this one, but Barabbas!"

Now Barabbas was a robber.

Chapter XIX

1THEN PILATE TOOK JESUS and flogged him. 2And the soldiers braided a crown of thorns, put it on his head, arrayed him in a purple robe, 3and came to him, saying, "Hail, Ruler of the Judeans!" And they struck Jesus with their hands.

4Pilate went outside again, and said to the people, "Behold, I am bringing Jesus out to you, that you may know that I find no crime in him."

5So Jesus came outside, wearing the thorny crown and the purple robe. Pilate said, "See the man!"

6When the chief priests and their attendants saw Jesus, they cried out, "Crucify, crucify!"

Pilate said to them, "Take him and crucify him yourselves, for I find no crime in him."

7The Judeans answered, "We have a law, and according to that law he ought to die, because he pretends to be the Child of God."

8When Pilate heard this said, he was more afraid, 9and entered the praetorium again and said to Jesus, "Where are you from?"

But Jesus gave no answer.

10Pilate therefore said to him, "You will not speak to me? Do you not know that I have the authority to release you, and the authority to crucify you?"

11Jesus answered, "You have no power over me unless it has been given you from above; therefore the one who delivered me to you has a greater sin."

12At this Pilate sought to release Jesus, but the Judeans cried out, "If you release this person, you are not Caesar's friend. For anyone who claims ruling power speaks against Caesar."

[13]Hearing these words, Pilate brought Jesus outside and sat on a judgment seat in a place called the Pavement, Gabbatha in Hebrew. [14]That was the day of preparation for the Passover, about the sixth hour. Pilate said to the Judeans, "See, your ruler!"

[15]They cried out, "Take him away! Take him away! Crucify him!"

Pilate said to them, "Shall I crucify your ruler?"

The chief priests answered, "We have no ruler except Caesar!" [16]Then Pilate delivered Jesus to them to be crucified. [17]The people took Jesus, and he went forth, carrying his own cross, to what was called the place of a skull, which is called in Hebrew Golgotha. [18]There they crucified Jesus, and with him two others, one on either side, and in the middle was Jesus. [19]Pilate also wrote a title and put it on the cross; it read, "Jesus of Nazareth, Ruler of the Judeans."

[20]This title was read by many of the Judeans, because the place where Jesus was crucified was near the city, and it was written in Hebrew, Latin, and Greek. [21]The chief priests of the Judeans said to Pilate, "Do not write, 'The Ruler of the Judeans,' but, 'This man said, I am Ruler of the Judeans.'"

[22]Pilate answered, "What I have written, I have written."

[23]When the soldiers crucified Jesus they took his garments and tunic and made four parts, one part for each soldier. But the tunic was without seam, woven from top to bottom, [24]so they said to one another, "Let us not tear it, but cast lots for it to see whose it shall be." This fulfilled the scripture: "They parted my garments among themselves, and for my clothing they cast lots." *(Ps 22:18)* [25]So the soldiers did this.

Standing by the cross of Jesus were his mother, and her sister, Mary of Clopas,* and Mary Magdalene. [26]When Jesus saw his mother, and the disciple whom he loved standing near, he said to her, "Woman, look, your son!" [27]Then Jesus said to the disciple, "Look, your mother!" And from that hour the disciple took her to his own home.

[28]After this, knowing that all was now finished, Jesus said (to fulfil the scripture), "I thirst."

[29]A bowl full of vinegar stood there, so they put a sponge full

*There is no indication as to what or whom Clopas might be.

of the vinegar on a hyssop and held it to his mouth. [30]When Jesus had received the vinegar, he said, "It is finished."

Bowing his head, Jesus surrendered his spirit.

[31]This was the day of preparation, and not wanting the bodies to remain on the cross on the Sabbath (for that Sabbath was a high day), the Judeans asked Pilate that their legs might be broken, and that they might be taken away. [32]So the soldiers came and broke the legs of the first and of the other crucified with him, [33]but when they came to Jesus and saw that he was already dead, they did not break his legs. [34]But one of the soldiers pierced his side with a spear, and at once there came out blood and water. [35]One who saw it was a witness and this testimony is true; the witness knows and tells the truth, that you also may believe. [36]For these things happened to fulfil the scripture, "Not a bone of the lamb shall be broken." *(Ex 12:46)* [37]And again another scripture says, "They shall see whom they have pierced." *(Zech 12:10)*

[38]After this Joseph of Arimathea, a disciple of Jesus, but secretly for fear of the Judeans, asked Pilate for permission to take away the body of Jesus, and Pilate allowed it. So Joseph came and took away the body of Jesus. [39]Nicodemus also, the one who had first come to Jesus by night, brought a mixture of myrrh and aloes, about a hundred pounds. [40]They took the body of Jesus, and wrapped it in sheets with the spices, according to the burial custom of the Judeans. [41]In the place where Jesus was crucified there was a garden, and in the garden a new tomb in which no one had yet been put. [42]So, because of the preparation of the Judeans, as the tomb was close at hand, they placed Jesus there.

Chapter XX

[1]NOW ON THE FIRST DAY of the week Mary Magdalene came early, while it was still dark, to the tomb and saw that the stone had been taken away from the tomb. [2]She ran and came to Simon Peter and the other disciple whom Jesus loved, and said to them, "They have taken the body of Jesus out of the tomb, and we do not know where they have put it."

[3]Peter started out with the other disciple, and they went to the

tomb. [4]They both ran together, but the other disciple ran more quickly than Peter and arrived at the tomb first. [5]Stooping to look in, he saw the cloths lying there; however, he did not enter.

[6]Simon Peter, following him, arrived and went into the tomb and saw the sheets lying there, [7]and the cloth which had been on his head, lying not with the other sheets but wrapped round in a place by itself. [8]Then the other disciple, who had arrived at the tomb first, also went in, and saw and believed. [9]As yet they did not know the scripture, that Jesus must rise from the dead. [10]The disciples then returned home.

[11]But Mary stood weeping outside the tomb. As she wept she stooped to look into the tomb, [12]and saw two angels in white, sitting where the body of Jesus had lain, one at the head and one at the feet. [13]They said to her, "Woman, why are you weeping?"

She said to them, "They have taken away the body of Jesus and I do not know where they have put it."

[14]Saying this, Mary turned round and saw Jesus standing there, but she did not know that it was Jesus, [15]who said, "Woman, why are you weeping? Whom do you seek?"

Thinking that it was the gardener, Mary said, "Sir, if you have carried the body somewhere, tell me where you have put it and I will take it away."

[16]Jesus said to her, "Mary."

She turned and said in Hebrew, "Rabboni!" (which means teacher).

[17]Jesus said to Mary, "Do not touch me for I have not yet returned to the one who sent me. But go to my sisters and brothers and tell them I am returning to the Source of my being, and the Source of your being, to my God and your God."

[18]Mary Magdalene went and announced to the disciples, "I have seen the Teacher." And she told them what Jesus had said to her.

[19]Early in the evening of that first day of the week, the doors being shut where the disciples were, because they feared the Judeans, Jesus came and stood in their midst and said, "Peace be with you."

[20]Having said this, Jesus showed them wounded hands and

side. Then the disciples rejoiced to see their leader. [21]Jesus said to them again, "Peace be with you. As God has sent me, I also send you."

[22]Saying this, Jesus breathed on them and said, "Receive the Holy Spirit. [23]If you forgive the sins of any, they have been forgiven; if you retain the sins of any, they have been retained."

[24]But Thomas, one of the twelve, called the Twin, was not with them when Jesus came. [25]So the other disciples told him, "We have seen the Teacher."

But Thomas said to them, "Unless I see where the nails were in his hands, and put my finger into the holes made by the nails, and put my hand into his side, I will not believe."

[26]Eight days later, again the disciples were in the house, and Thomas was with them. While the doors were shut, Jesus came and stood in their midst and said, "Peace be with you."

[27]Then Jesus said to Thomas, "Put your finger here and perceive my hands, and hold out your hand, and put it into my side, and do not be faithless, but faithful."

[28]Thomas answered, "My Ruler and my God!"

[29]Jesus said to Thomas, "Have you believed only because you have seen me? Blessed are those who believe without seeing."

[30]Jesus did many other signs in the presence of the disciples, which are not written in this book. [31]But these have been written that you may believe that Jesus is the Christ, the Child of God, and that believing you may have life in the name of Jesus.

Chapter XXI

[1]AFTER THIS Jesus appeared again to the disciples by the Sea of Tiberias. It happened this way: [2]Simon Peter, Thomas called the Twin, Nathanael of Cana in Galilee, the sons of Zebedee, and two other disciples were together. [3]Simon Peter said to them, "I am going fishing."

They said, "We will also go with you." They went and set out in the boat, but that night they caught nothing.

[4]Early in the morning, Jesus stood on the shore; however the disciples did not know that it was Jesus. [5]Jesus said to them, "Chil-

dren, have you any fish?"

They answered, "No."

^{6}Jesus said, "Cast the net on the right side of the boat, and you will find some." They did so, and were no longer able to drag it in because of the quantity of fish.

^{7}The disciple whom Jesus loved said to Peter, "It is the Teacher."

Hearing that it was Jesus, Simon Peter put on a garment, for he had been naked, and leaped into the sea. ^{8}But the other disciples came in the small boat, dragging the net full of fish, for they were not far from the land, only about a hundred yards off. ^{9}When they landed they saw a charcoal fire there with fish lying on it, also bread.

^{10}Jesus said to them, "Bring some of the fish that you have caught."

^{11}Simon Peter went aboard and dragged ashore the net full of large fish, a hundred and fifty-three of them; yet with so many fish, the net was not torn.

^{12}Jesus said to them, "Come and have breakfast."

None of the disciples dared to question, "Who are you?" They knew it was their Teacher. ^{13}Jesus came and took the bread and gave it to them, and so with the fish. ^{14}This was now the third manifestation to the disciples of Jesus raised from the dead.

^{15}When they had finished breakfast, Jesus said to Simon Peter, "Simon, son of John, do you love* me more than these?"

Peter answered, "Yes, Teacher, you know that I love** you."

Jesus said, "Feed my lambs."

^{16}A second time Jesus said, "Simon, son of John, do you love* me?"

Peter answered, "Yes, Teacher, you know that I love** you."

Jesus said, "Shepherd my little sheep."

^{17}Jesus said the third time, "Simon, son of John, do you love** me?"

Peter was grieved that Jesus said to him the third time, "Do you love** me?" and answered, "Teacher, you know all things; you know that I love** you."

Jesus said, "Feed my little sheep.

*agape
**filio

¹⁸"Thus truly, I tell you, when you were younger, you girded yourself and walked where you wished; but when you grow old, you will stretch out your hands, and another will gird you and will carry you where you do not want to go." ¹⁹(Jesus said this to signify by what death Peter would glorify God.) And after saying this Jesus said to Peter, "Follow me."

²⁰Turning, Peter saw following them the disciple whom Jesus loved*, the one who had leaned on Jesus's breast at the supper and had said, "Sir, who is the one who will betray you?" ²¹Seeing this disciple, Peter said to Jesus, "Teacher, what about this one?"

²²Jesus said, "If I want this one to remain until I come, what is that to you? Follow me!"

²³The saying spread abroad among the sisters and brothers that this disciple was not to die; but Jesus did not say that the disciple was not to die, but, "If I want this one to remain until I come, what is that to you?"

²⁴This is the disciple witnessing concerning these things, and who wrote these things, and we know that this testimony is true.

²⁵But there are also many other things that Jesus did; if they each were written, I think that the world itself could not contain the books written.

*agape

The Gospel According to Mark

Chapter I

[1]THE BEGINNING of the gospel of Jesus Christ:

[2]As it is written in Isaiah the prophet, "Behold, I send my messenger ahead of you, who shall prepare your road; *(Mal 3:1)* [3]a voice of one crying in the desert: Prepare God's road, make the paths straight." *(Is 40:3)*

[4]John the baptizer came in the desert proclaiming a baptism of repentance for forgiveness of sins. [5]People of all the country of Judea and all the Jerusalemites went out to him, and, confessing their sins, they were baptized by John in the Jordan River. [6]John was clothed in camel's hair, with a leather girdle around his waist, and he ate locusts and wild honey. [7]John proclaimed this: "After me comes one who is more powerful than I, the thong of whose sandals I am not competent to stoop down and untie. [8]I have baptized you in water, but the expected one will baptize you in the holy spirit."

[9]It happened then that Jesus came from Nazareth of Galilee and was baptized in the Jordan River by John. [10]When Jesus came up out of the water, immediately it was seen that the heavens tore open and the spirit like a dove descended upon Jesus; [11]a voice came out of the heavens, saying, "You are my child, my beloved. I am well pleased with you."

[12]The spirit immediately drove Jesus forth into the desert. [13]And Jesus was in the desert forty days, tempted by Satan, and was with the wild beasts, and was ministered to by angels. [14]Now after John was imprisoned, Jesus came into Galilee, proclaiming the good news of God, [15]and saying, "The time has been fulfilled, and the power of God is near; repent, and believe in the good news."

[16]And passing along by the Sea of Galilee, Jesus saw Simon and Andrew the brother of Simon casting a net in the sea, for their

trade was fishing. [17]And Jesus said to them, "Come along with me and I will make you become fishers of women and men."

[18]Immediately leaving the nets they followed Jesus. [19]And going on a little farther, Jesus saw James the son of Zebedee and John the brother of James, who were in the ship mending nets. [20]And immediately Jesus called them, and leaving their father Zebedee in the ship with the hired servants, they went along with Jesus.

[21]And they entered Capernaum, and immediately on the sabbath Jesus entered the synagogue and taught. [22]People were astounded at his teaching, for Jesus taught them as one having authority, and not as the scribes. [23]At that moment there was in their synagogue a man with an unclean spirit, [24]and he cried out, "What have you to do with us, Jesus of Nazareth? Have you come to destroy us? I know who you are, the holy one of God."

[25]Jesus rebuked the spirit saying, "Be silent, and come out of him!"

[26]And the unclean spirit, shaking the man and shouting with a loud voice, came out of him. [27]All were astounded, so that they debated among themselves, saying, "What is this? Teaching a new thing with authority, and commanding unclean spirits, and they obey him!"

[28]And immediately the report about Jesus went forth everywhere, into all the neighborhood of Galilee.

[29]Jesus left the synagogue, and immediately came into the house of Simon and Andrew, with James and John. [30]Now Simon's mother-in-law lay sick with a fever, and immediately they told Jesus about her. [31]Jesus approached her, held her hand, and lifted her; the fever left her and she served them.

[32]When evening came, as the sun was setting, they brought to Jesus all those who had sickness or were possessed with demons. [33]And the whole city assembled at the door. [34]Jesus healed many who were sick with various diseases, expelled many demons, and did not allow the demons to speak, because the demons knew Jesus.

[35]Early in the morning, before daylight, Jesus got up and went out away from there to a desert place, and there prayed. [36]And Simon and those with him hunted for Jesus. [37]When they found

him, they said, "Everyone is looking for you."

38 Jesus said to them, "Let us go elsewhere into the neighboring towns, that I may speak there also, for I came to do this."

39 Jesus came, speaking in the synagogues, and expelling demons, throughout all Galilee.

40 A leper, begging, came and knelt before Jesus and said, "If you are willing, you can cleanse me."

41 Filled with tenderness, Jesus stretched out his hand, touched the leper and said, "I am willing; be cleansed."

42 Immediately the leprosy left, and the leper was clean. 43 And Jesus sternly admonished and sent the one who had been a leper out immediately, 44 saying, "See that you tell no one anything, but go, show yourself to the priests, and offer for your cleansing what Moses commanded, for a testimony to them."

45 But the former leper went out and began to proclaim many things and to spread the news, so that Jesus could no longer openly enter a city, but was outside in desert places. People came to Jesus from all directions.

Chapter II

1 AFTER SOME DAYS, Jesus returned to Capernaum and it was reported that he was at home. 2 Many gathered there, so that there was no longer space even near the door. And Jesus proclaimed the word to them. 3 Then four people came, carrying a paralytic to Jesus. 4 Not being able to get near Jesus because of the crowd, they removed the roof above him, and when they had made an opening, they let down the mat on which the paralytic lay. 5 Seeing their faith, Jesus said to the paralytic, "My child, your sins are forgiven."

6 Now some of the scribes were sitting there and contemplating in their hearts, 7 "Why does this person say such a thing? It is blasphemy! Who can forgive sins but the one God?"

8 Jesus, immediately perceiving in his spirit that they thus deliberated among themselves, said to them, "Why do you debate these things in your hearts? 9 Which is easier, to say to the paralytic, 'Your sins are forgiven,' or to say, 'Rise, take up your mat and

walk'? ¹⁰But that you may know that Humanity's Child has authority on earth to forgive sins—'' Jesus said to the paralytic, ¹¹''I tell you, stand up, take your mat and go to your house.''

¹²The paralytic stood up, immediately took up the mat, and went forth before them all; so that they were all amazed and glorified God, saying, ''We never saw such a thing!''

¹³Jesus went forth again beside the sea, and the whole crowd came to him, and he taught them. ¹⁴As he walked along Jesus saw Levi the son of Alphaeus sitting in the tax collectors' place, and said to Levi, ''Follow me.'' And Levi stood up and followed Jesus.

¹⁵Presently, as Jesus reclined at table in his house, many tax collectors and sinners reclined there with Jesus and his disciples; for there were many who followed Jesus. ¹⁶And the scribes of the Pharisees, when they saw that Jesus ate with sinners and tax collectors, said to his disciples, ''Does Jesus eat with tax collectors and sinners?''

¹⁷Hearing this, Jesus said to them, ''Those who are well do not need a physician, but sick people do. I did not come to call righteous people, but sinners.''

¹⁸When John's disciples and the Pharisees were fasting, people came and said to Jesus, ''Why do John's disciples and the disciples of the Pharisees fast, but your disciples do not fast?''

¹⁹And Jesus said to them, ''Do wedding guests fast while the bride and bridegroom are with them? While they have the bride and bridegroom with them they cannot fast. ²⁰But the days will come when the bride and bridegroom are taken away from them, and then they will fast on that day.

²¹''No one sews a patch of unshrunk cloth on an old garment; otherwise the new patch shrinks away from the old and a worse tear is made. ²²And no one puts new wine into old wineskins; otherwise, the wine will burst the wineskins, and the wine is lost, along with the wineskins. New wine is for fresh wineskins.''

²³One sabbath Jesus was walking through the grainfields, and his disciples, making their way, began to pluck ears of grain. ²⁴And the Pharisees said to him, ''Look, why are they doing what is not lawful on the sabbath?''

²⁵And Jesus said to them, ''Have you never read what David

did, when he was in need and hungry, as were those with him, [26]how David entered the house of God, when Abiathar was high priest, and ate the bread of presentation which is not lawful for any except priests to eat, and gave it to those who were with him?''

[27]Then Jesus said to them, ''The sabbath was made for the sake of people, not people for the sake of the sabbath; [28]so the Child of Humanity is also ruler of the sabbath.''

Chapter III

[1]AGAIN JESUS ENTERED a synagogue, and a man was there who had a withered hand. [2]And others watched carefully to see whether Jesus would heal someone on the sabbath, so that they might accuse him. [3]And Jesus said to the person with the withered hand, ''Stand up here.''

[4]And to the others Jesus said, ''Is it lawful on the sabbath to do good or to do evil, to save a life or to kill?''

But they were silent. [5]And looking around at them with anger, and being greatly grieved at their hardness of heart, Jesus said to the man, ''Stretch out your hand.''

He stretched it out, and the hand was restored. [6]The Pharisees went out immediately with the Herodians and conspired against Jesus that they might destroy him.

[7]Jesus departed with his disciples to the sea, and a large crowd from Galilee followed, along with people from Judea, [8]Jerusalem, Idumea, and beyond the Jordan, and around Tyre and Sidon. The crowd, hearing of all that he did, came to Jesus. [9]And he told the disciples to keep a boat near by because of the crowd, lest they should crush him. [10]Jesus had healed so many, that all who had diseases pushed toward him to touch him. [11]And whenever the unclean spirits saw Jesus, they fell down before him and cried out, ''You are the Child of God.'' [12]And Jesus strictly warned them not to make him known.

[13]Jesus went up onto the mountain, called those whom he desired, and they went to him. [14]He appointed twelve to accompany him, to be sent out to proclaim the message, [15]and to have authority to cast out demons. [16]The twelve were: Simon, given the

name of Peter; [17]James the son of Zebedee and John the brother of James, to whom Jesus added the name Boanerges, or sons of thunder; [18]Andrew, Philip, Bartholomew, Matthew, Thomas, James the son of Alphaeus, Thaddaeus, Simon the Canaanean, [19]and Judas Iscariot, who betrayed Jesus.

Then Jesus went to a house, [20]and the crowd gathered again, so that they could not even eat their bread. [21]And when those with him heard it, they went forth to seize him, for they said, "Jesus is beside himself."

[22]Scribes who had come down from Jerusalem said, "He belongs to Be-elzebub, and by the ruler of the demons casts out demons."

[23]Calling them together, Jesus spoke to them in parables, "How can Satan throw Satan out? [24]If a nation is divided against itself, that nation cannot stand. [25]And if a house is divided against itself, that house will not be able to stand. [26]And if Satan stands up against Satan and is divided, Satan cannot stand, but comes to an end. [27]No one can enter a strong person's house and plunder the goods, without first binding the strong owner; then indeed the house may be plundered.

[28]Truly, I tell you that all will be forgiven to humanity's children, their sins and whatever blasphemies they utter. [29]But whoever blasphemes against the Holy Spirit will never be forgiven, but is guilty of eternal sin." [30](Referring to their saying, "He has an unclean spirit.")

[31]The mother, brothers, and sisters of Jesus came, and standing outside they sent a message and called to him. [32]And a crowd was sitting around him, and they said to Jesus, "Your mother and your brothers and sisters are outside, asking for you."

[33]And Jesus replied, "Who are my mother and brothers and sisters?" [34]Looking at those sitting in the circle around him, Jesus said, "Here are my mother and my sister and my brother! [35]Whoever does the will of God is my brother, sister, and mother."

Chapter IV

[1]AGAIN JESUS BEGAN to teach beside the sea, and a very large

crowd assembled around him, so he got into a boat and sat in it on the sea; and the crowd was beside the sea on the land. [2]Jesus taught them many things in parables, and in his teaching said to them, [3]"Listen, a planter went out to plant seeds, [4]and in the planting, some seed fell along the path, and birds came and devoured it. [5]Other seed fell on rocky ground, where it had not much soil, and immediately it sprang up, because it had so little depth of soil; [6]but when the sun rose it was scorched, and having no root it withered. [7]Other seed fell among some thorns and the thorns grew up and choked it, and it yielded nothing. [8]Other seed fell into good soil and it came up and grew and brought forth fruits, thirty and sixty and a hundred."

[9]And Jesus said, "Those who have ears to hear, let them listen."

[10]When Jesus was alone, those around him with the twelve asked about the parables. [11]And Jesus said to them, "The mystery of the dominion of God has been given to you, but for those outside everything is in parables. [12]For seeing, they see but do not perceive, and hearing, they hear but do not understand; otherwise they would turn and be forgiven."

[13]And Jesus said to them, "Do you not understand this parable? Then how will you understand other parables? [14]The planter sows the word. [15]Now these are the ones along the path where the word is planted, and when they hear, immediately Satan comes and takes the word which was planted in them. [16]And these are likewise the ones planted upon rocky ground, who, when they hear the word, immediately receive it with joy, [17]but having no root in themselves, are short lived. Then, when affliction or persecution comes on account of the word, immediately they are overcome. [18]And others are the ones planted among thorns; they are those who hear the word, [19]but the cares of the world, and deceitfulness of riches, and desires for other things come in and choke the word, and it becomes unfruitful. [20]But those that were planted in the good soil are the ones who hear the word and welcome it and bear fruit, thirty and sixty and a hundred."

[21]And Jesus said to them, "Is a lamp intended to be put under a bushel? or under a bed? and not on a lamp stand? [22]For there is

nothing hidden except to be made manifest, nor is anything covered, but to be shown openly. [23]Those who have ears to hear, let them listen."

[24]Jesus then said, "Attend to what you hear. By the measure you measure, it will be measured to you, and more will be added to you. [25]For the one who has will be given more, and from the one who has not, even what that one has will be taken away."

[26]And Jesus said, "Thus is the realm of God: as if a person might scatter seed upon the ground, [27]and might sleep and rise night and day, and the seed sprouts and grows, no one knows how. [28]From itself the earth produces fruit, first a blade, then an ear, then full grain in the ear. [29]But when the fruit is ripe, immediately one puts forth the sickle, because the harvest has come."

[30]And Jesus said, "How shall we compare the realm of God, or what parable shall we use? [31]It is like a grain of mustard seed, which when sown upon the ground, is the smallest of all seeds on earth; [32]yet when it is sown and grows up it becomes the largest of all herbs, and puts forth great branches, so that birds of the heavens can live in its shade."

[33]In many such parables Jesus spoke the word to them, as they were able to hear it; [34]he never spoke to them without a parable, but privately to his own disciples Jesus explained all things.

[35]On that day, when evening had come, Jesus said to them, "Let us cross over to the other side."

[36]And leaving the crowd, they took Jesus with them, as he was in the boat. And other boats were with him. [37]And a great storm of wind arose, and the waves beat into the boat, so that the boat was already filling. [38]Jesus was in the stern, asleep on a pillow, and they woke him and said, "Teacher, does it not matter to you that we are perishing?"

[39]When awakened, Jesus rebuked the wind, and said to the sea, "Hush! Be still!"

[40]The wind dropped, and there was a great calm.

[41]Jesus said to them, "Why are you afraid? Have you no faith?"

[42]And they feared a great fear, and said to one another, "Who is this person, that both wind and sea obey him?"

Chapter V

¹THEY CAME TO THE OTHER SIDE of the sea, to the country of the Gerasenes. ²Leaving the boat, Jesus met a man coming out of the tombs, a man with an unclean spirit, ³who lived among the tombs for no one was able to bind him any more with a chain. ⁴For he had often been bound with fetters and chains, but he burst the chains and broke the fetters, and no one was able to subdue him. ⁵Night and day among the tombs and on the mountains he was always crying out and cutting himself with stones.

⁶Seeing Jesus from afar, the man ran and worshiped him, ⁷and crying out with a loud voice, said, "What have you to do with me, Jesus, Child of the Most High God? I adjure you by God, do not torment me."

⁸For Jesus said to him, "Come out of this man, you unclean spirit!"

⁹Then Jesus asked, "What is your name?"

The spirit replied, "My name is Legion, for we are many." ¹⁰And the spirit begged Jesus not to send them outside the country.

¹¹Now a large herd of pigs was feeding near there on the hillside, ¹²and the spirits begged Jesus, "Send us into the pigs, let us enter them."

¹³So Jesus allowed this. And the unclean spirits came out and entered the pigs, then the herd of about two thousand rushed down the precipice into the sea, and were drowned in the sea.

¹⁴Those feeding them fled, and told it in the city and in the country. And people came to see what it was that had happened. ¹⁵And they came to Jesus, and saw the demoniac who had had the legion sitting there, clothed and in his right mind, and they were afraid. ¹⁶And those who had seen it told what had happened to the demoniac and to the pigs. ¹⁷Then the people began to beg Jesus to depart from their neighborhood.

¹⁸As Jesus was getting into the boat, the man who had been possessed with demons begged to go with Jesus. ¹⁹But Jesus would not permit it, and said to him, "Go home to your friends, and tell them that God has done these things for you, and has had pity on you."

^{20}And the man went away and began to proclaim in Decapolis the things Jesus had done for him. And everyone was amazed.

^{21}And when Jesus had again crossed in the boat to the other side, a large crowd gathered about him beside the sea. ^{22}Then came Jairus, a ruler of the synagogue, and seeing Jesus, Jairus fell at his feet, ^{23}and begged him, saying, "My daughter is at the point of death. Come and lay your hands on her, so that she may be healed and live."

^{24}Jesus went with Jairus, and a large crowd followed and pressed about Jesus. ^{25}There was a woman who had had a flow of blood for twelve years, ^{26}and who had endured much under many physicians, and had spent all that she had and had gained nothing but rather grew worse. ^{27}Having heard the reports about Jesus she approached behind him in the crowd and touched his garment. ^{28}For she said, "If I may touch even his garments, I shall be healed."

^{29}And immediately the bleeding stopped, and she knew in her body that she was cured of the disease. ^{30}Immediately Jesus, knowing in himself that power had gone forth out of him, turned around in the crowd, and said, "Who touched my garments?"

^{31}And his disciples said to him, "You see the crowd pressing around you, and yet you say, 'Who touched me?'"

^{32}Jesus looked around to see who had done this. ^{33}And the woman, fearing and trembling, knowing what had happened to her, came and fell before him and told Jesus the whole truth. ^{34}And Jesus said to her, "Daughter, your faith has healed you. Go in peace and be whole, without disease."

^{35}While Jesus was still speaking, some came from the house of the ruler of the synagogue, saying, "Your daughter is dead. Why trouble the Teacher any further?"

^{36}But hearing what they said, Jesus said to Jairus the ruler of the synagogue, "Do not fear, only trust."

^{37}And Jesus allowed no one to accompany him except Peter, James, and John the brother of James. ^{38}When they came to the house of the ruler of the synagogue, seeing the tumult, the people weeping and wailing loudly, ^{39}Jesus entered and said to them, "Why do you make an uproar and weep? The child is not dead but sleeping.''

[40]And they ridiculed Jesus. But he put them all outside, and took the child's father and mother and those with him, and went in where the child was. [41]Taking hold of the child's hand Jesus said to her, "Talitha cumi," which means, "Little girl, stand up."

[42]And immediately the girl stood up and walked, for she was twelve years old. At that moment their amazement was overwhelming. [43]Jesus demanded that no one should know this, and told them to give her something to eat.

Chapter VI

[1]JESUS WENT AWAY from there and came to his native place, and his disciples followed him. [2]On the next sabbath Jesus began to teach in the synagogue, and many who listened were astonished, saying, "Where did this man get these things? What wisdom is given to him? and such powerful works come about through his hands! [3]Is this not the carpenter, the son of Mary and brother of James, Joses, Judas, and Simon? And are his sisters not here with us?"

The people were angered by him. [4]And Jesus said to them, "Prophets are not without honor, except in their native places, among their own relatives, and in their own houses."

[5]And Jesus could do no powerful works there, except to lay hands upon a few sick people and heal them. [6]And he marveled because of their unbelief.

Jesus went about teaching among the villages in circuit.

[7]Calling to himself the twelve, Jesus began to send them out two by two, and gave them authority over unclean spirits, [8]and charged them to take nothing on the road except a staff, (neither bread, nor a wallet, nor coins in their belts) [9]to put on sandals but not two tunics. [10]And Jesus said to them, "Where you enter a house, stay there until you leave the place. [11]And whatever place does not receive you and refuses to hear you, when you leave, shake off the dust from under your feet for a testimony against them."

[12]Going forth they proclaimed that people should repent. [13]They cast out many demons, and anointed with oil many that

were sick and healed them.

14King Herod heard of Jesus, for his name had become known. Some said, "John the baptizer has been raised from the dead; therefore powerful works operate in this person."

15But others said, "It is Elijah."

And others said, "A prophet, like one of our prophets."

16But when Herod heard of it he said, "John, whom I beheaded, has been raised."

17For Herod had sent and seized John, and bound him in prison, because of Herodias, his brother Philip's wife; because Herod had married Herodias. 18For John said to Herod, "It is not lawful for you to have the wife of your brother."

19Now Herodias had a grudge against John and wanted to kill him, but could not. 20Herod feared John, and knowing that he was a just and holy person, kept him safe. Hearing John made Herod very uncomfortable, and yet he heard him gladly. 21But an opportune time came when Herod gave a festive supper on his birthday for his courtiers and chiliarchs and the chief people of Galilee. 22For when Herodias' daughter came in and danced, she pleased Herod and those reclining at supper, and the king said to the girl, "Ask me for whatever you wish, and I will give it to you." 23And Herod made a vow to her, "Whatever you ask me, I will give you, up to half of my possessions."

24She went out and said to her mother, "What may I ask?"

And Herodias said, "The head of John the baptizer."

25The dancer came in immediately with haste to the king, and asked, saying, "I want you to give me at once, on a dish, the head of John the Baptist."

26And the king became deeply grieved; but because of the oaths and the guests present he did not want to reject her. 27And immediately the king sent an executioner and gave the order to bring the head. The executioner went and beheaded John in the prison, 28and brought the head on a dish, and gave it to the girl; the girl gave it to her mother. 29When John's disciples heard of it they came and took the body, and laid it in a tomb.

30The apostles gathered round Jesus and reported all the things which they had done and had taught. 31Jesus said to them, "Come away by yourselves privately to a desert place, and rest a little."

For many were coming and going, and they had no opportunity even to eat. [32]So they went away in the boat to a desert place by themselves. [33]Now many people saw them going, and knew them, and they ran there on foot from all the towns, and arrived there ahead of them. [34]At the landing Jesus saw a large crowd, and had compassion on them, because they were like sheep without a shepherd, and Jesus began to teach them many things.

[35]When it grew late, the disciples approached and said, "This is a desert place, and the hour is now late; [36]dismiss the crowd that they may go to the fields and villages round about and buy themselves something to eat."

[37]But Jesus answered them, "You give them something to eat."

And they replied, "Shall we go and buy two hundred denarii worth of bread, and give it to them to eat?"

[38]And Jesus said to them, "How many loaves have you? Go and see."

But, already knowing, they said, "Five, and two fish."

[39]Then Jesus instructed them all to recline by company on the green grass. [40]So they reclined by groups, by hundreds and by fifties. [41]And taking the five loaves and the two fish, and looking up to heaven, Jesus blessed and broke the loaves, and gave them to the disciples to set before the people. And Jesus divided the two fish among them all. [42]They all ate and were satisfied. [43]And they took up twelve baskets full of broken bread and of the fish. [44]And those who ate the loaves numbered five thousand.

[45]Immediately Jesus made his disciples embark in the boat and go before him to the other side, to Bethsaida, while he dismissed the crowd. [46]And having said farewell to them, Jesus went to the mountain to pray. [47]And when evening came, the boat was out on the sea, and Jesus was alone on the land. [48]And seeing that they were distressed in rowing, for the wind was against them, about the fourth watch of the night Jesus came to them, walking on the sea, and meaning to pass by them. [49]But when they saw him walking on the sea, they thought it was a ghost and screamed, [50]for they all saw him, and were frightened. But immediately Jesus talked to them and said, "Have courage, I am here, do not be afraid."

[51]Jesus got into the boat with them and the wind ceased. They were thoroughly amazed within themselves, [52]for they did not understand about the loaves, and their hearts were hardened.

[53]Having crossed the water, they came to Genesaret, and anchored there. [54]And when they got out of the boat, immediately the people recognized Jesus [55]and ran about the whole countryside and began to carry sick people on their mats to any place where they heard he was. [56]And wherever Jesus came, in villages, cities, or country, they laid the sick people in the market places and begged him that they might touch even the fringe of his garment, and all who touched Jesus were made well.

Chapter VII

[1]THE PHARISEES GATHERED around Jesus, with some of the scribes who had come from Jerusalem, [2]and they noticed that some of his disciples ate bread with dirty, that is unwashed, hands. [3]For the Pharisees and all the Judeans do not eat without washing their hands, in accordance with the tradition of the elders. [4]And coming from the market place they do not eat before pouring water over their hands, and there are many other traditions to which they hold, such as immersion of cups and utensils and bronze kettles. [5]The Pharisees and the scribes questioned Jesus, "Why do your disciples not act according to the tradition of the elders, but eat with dirty hands?"

[6]Jesus said to them, "Isaiah prophesied well concerning your hypocrisies, as it is written, 'This people honors me with their lips, but their heart is far from me; [7]in vain they worship me, teaching doctrines which are merely commands of human beings. [8]Abandoning the commandment of God, you cling to human traditions.'" *(Is 29:13)*

[9]Jesus continued, saying, "How readily you have set aside the commandment of God to keep your own tradition! [10]For Moses said, 'Honor your father and your mother'; and 'Let any one who speaks evil of father or mother end in death'; [11]But you say, 'If a person says to father or mother, What you might have received from me is Corban' (that is, given to God), [12]then you no longer

permit that person to do anything for either father or mother, [13]thus annulling the word of God by your own tradition which you accept. And many similar things you do.''

[14]And calling together the crowd again, Jesus said to them, "Listen to me, all of you, and understand: [15]there is nothing from outside a person which by entering can defile that person, but the things coming forth out of people are what defile them.''

[17]When Jesus had entered a house, away from the crowd, the disciples questioned him about the parable. [18]And Jesus answered, "Are you also undiscerning? Do you not understand that whatever enters the body from outside cannot defile the person, [19]because it does not enter the heart but the stomach, and so passes out of the body.'' (Thus Jesus declared all foods clean.) [20]And Jesus said, "What comes forth out of a person is what defiles. [21]For from within, from people's hearts, come evil thoughts, fornications, thefts, murders, adulteries, [22]greed, wickedness, deceit, lewdness, an evil eye, blasphemy, arrogance, and foolishness. [23]All these evil things come from within, and they defile people.''

[24]From there Jesus went away to the region of Tyre. Entering a house there, he wished no one to know it, but Jesus could not be hid.

[25]Immediately a woman whose daughter had an unclean spirit heard of him and came and fell at Jesus' feet. [26]The woman was a Greek, a Syrophoenician by race, and she asked Jesus to cast the demon out of her daughter.

[27]Jesus said to her, "Let the children be satisfied first, for it is not good to take the children's bread and throw it to the dogs.''

[28]She answered him, saying, "Yes, Sir, and yet the dogs under the table eat the children's crumbs.''

[29]Jesus replied, "Because of this word, go along, for the demon has gone out of your daughter.''

[30]And the woman went home, and found the child lying on the couch, and the demon gone.

[31]Departing from the region of Tyre, Jesus went through Sidon to the Sea of Galilee, into the region of Decapolis. [32]And they brought to Jesus a man who was deaf and had difficulty speaking, and they begged Jesus to put his hand upon the deaf person.

[33]Taking him aside from the crowd privately, Jesus put his fingers into the man's ears, and spitting, touched his tongue. [34]Looking up to heaven, Jesus groaned, and said to the man, "Ephphatha," which means "Be opened." [35]And the man's ears were opened, his tongue was released, and he spoke correctly.

[36]Jesus ordered them to tell no one, but the more he ordered them, the more zealously they proclaimed it. [37]And they were most exceedingly astonished, saying, "Jesus has done all things well, and even makes the deaf hear and the mute speak."

Chapter VIII

[1]IN THOSE DAYS, when again a large crowd had assembled, and they had nothing left to eat, Jesus called his disciples to him, and said to them, [2]"I have compassion on the crowd, because they have now stayed with me three days, and have nothing to eat. [3]If I send them away hungry to their homes, they will faint on the way, and some of them have come from far away."

[4]And the disciples answered, "How can any one satisfy the hunger of these people with bread here in a desert?"

[5]Jesus asked them, "How many loaves have you?"

They said, "Seven."

[6]Then Jesus commanded the crowd to sit down on the ground, and taking the seven loaves and giving thanks, he broke them and gave them to his disciples that they might distribute them, and they served the whole crowd. [7]They also had a few fish, and blessing these Jesus told them that these also should be distributed. [8]And they all ate and were satisfied, and took up seven baskets of extra pieces. [9]The crowd numbered about four thousand. Jesus then dismissed them.

[10]Immediately he embarked in the boat with his disciples and went to the region of Dalmanutha.

[11]There the Pharisees came forward and began to debate with Jesus, seeking a heavenly sign from him, and testing him. [12]Groaning in spirit, Jesus said, "Why does this generation seek a sign? Truly, I tell you, will this generation be given a sign!"

[13]Leaving them, Jesus departed in the boat to the other side.

^{14}Now they forgot to take bread in the boat. Except for one loaf they had none with them. ^{15}Jesus charged them saying, "Watch out, beware of the leaven of the Pharisees and the leaven of Herod."

^{16}And they argued with one another, because they had no bread. ^{17}Knowing this, Jesus said to them, "Why do you argue about having no bread? Do you not yet perceive or understand? Are your hearts hardened? ^{18}Having eyes do you not see, and having ears do you not hear? And do you not remember? ^{19}When I broke the five loaves for the five thousand, how many baskets full of fragments did you collect?"

They answered, "Twelve."

^{20}"When the seven for the four thousand, how many baskets heaping with fragments did you collect?"

And they answered, "Seven."

^{21}Jesus then said, "Do you not yet perceive?"

^{22}Then they arrived at Bethsaida, and people brought a blind man and begged Jesus to touch him. ^{23}Taking the blind man by the hand, Jesus led him out of the village. Having spit on the blind eyes, Jesus put his hands upon the man and questioned him, "Do you see anything?"

^{24}And the man looked up and said, "I see people that look like walking trees."

^{25}Then again Jesus put his hands upon the eyes, and the man looked steadily and was restored, and saw everything clearly. ^{26}And Jesus sent the man home, saying, "You must not enter the village."

^{27}Jesus and his disciples went on to the villages of Caesarea Philippi. On the way Jesus questioned the disciples, saying, "Who do people say that I am?"

^{28}And they answered, "John the Baptist, or others say Elijah, and others one of the prophets."

^{29}And Jesus questioned them, "But you, who do you say that I am?"

Peter answered, "You are the Christ."

^{30}Jesus warned them to tell no one about him.

^{31}Then Jesus began to teach them that it would be necessary for

Humanity's Child to suffer many things, to be rejected by the elders and chief priests and scribes, to be killed, and after three days to rise again. [32]Jesus spoke the word clearly. Then Peter, taking him aside, began to rebuke Jesus. [33]But Jesus, turning round and seeing the disciples, rebuked Peter, and said, "Get behind me, Satan! For you are not attending to the concerns of God, but the concerns of people."

[34]Calling together the crowd with his disciples, Jesus said to them, "If you wish to come after me, you must deny yourself and take up your cross and follow me. [35]For if you wish to preserve your life you will lose it. But all who lose their lives for the sake of me and the good news will save their lives. [36]For what does it profit a person to gain the whole world at the cost of his or her life? [37]And what could you pay in exchange for your life?

[38]"All who are ashamed of me and of my words in this adulterous and sinful generation, of them Humanity's Child will also be ashamed, on arrival in the glory of God with the holy angels."

Chapter IX

[1]JESUS SAID TO THEM, "Truly, I tell you, there are some standing here who will not taste death until they see the dominion of God come with power."

[2]After six days Jesus took Peter and James and John, and secretly led them to a high mountain by themselves. There Jesus was transformed before them, [3]and his garments became gleaming, intensely white, as no fuller on earth could whiten them. [4]And Elijah and Moses appeared to them, and they were conversing with Jesus. [5]Then Peter said to Jesus, "Rabbi, it is good that we are here; let us make three shelters, one for you and one for Moses and one for Elijah." ([6]Peter did not know what he was saying, for they were all extremely frightened.)

[7]There came a cloud overshadowing them, and a voice came out of the cloud, "This is my beloved Child, listen to him." [8]And suddenly looking around they no longer saw anyone except Jesus alone with them.

[9]And as they came down the mountain, Jesus commanded them

to tell no one what they had seen, except when Humanity's Child should rise from the dead. [10]So they kept the word to themselves, debating what "rising from the dead" meant.

[11]The three questioned Jesus, saying, "Why do the scribes say that Elijah of necessity must come first?"

[12]And Jesus answered, "Elijah coming first will indeed restore all things, and it is written that the Child of Humanity will suffer many things and be considered nothing. [13]But I tell you that, in fact, Elijah has come, and they did to him what they wished, as it was written of him."

[14]And when they came back to the other disciples, they saw a large crowd about them, and scribes debating with them. [15]And immediately the whole crowd, when they saw Jesus, were greatly amazed, and ran up and greeted him. [16]And Jesus questioned them, "What are you discussing with them?"

[17]And one of the crowd answered, "Teacher, I brought my son to you, for he has a mute spirit, [18]and wherever it seizes it rips him, foams, and grinds his teeth, and his health declines. I asked your disciples to cast it out, but they could not."

[19]Jesus answered them, "O faithless generation, how long will I be with you? How long will I bear with you? Bring the boy to me."

[20]And they brought him to Jesus, and seeing Jesus, the spirit violently convulsed the boy, who then fell on the ground and wallowed about, foaming at the mouth. [21]And Jesus asked the boy's father, "How long has this been happening to him?"

And he answered, "From childhood. [22]And it has often thrown him into the fires and into the water, to destroy him. But if you can do anything, have compassion and help us."

[23]Jesus responded, "If you can! All things are possible to one who believes."

[24]Immediately the father of the child cried out saying, "I believe. Help my unbelief!"

[25]Then Jesus, seeing that a crowd came running together, rebuked the unclean spirit, saying to it, "You mute and deaf spirit, I command you, come out of him, and never enter him again."

[26]And after crying out and convulsing him terribly, it came out,

and the boy appeared to be dead, so that many said that he died. ^{27}But Jesus, taking him by the hand, lifted the boy and he stood up.

^{28}When they entered a house, the disciples asked Jesus privately, "Why could we not cast it out?"

^{29}Jesus replied, "This kind cannot be driven out by anything but prayer."

^{30}Leaving there they passed through Galilee, and Jesus did not want anyone to know, ^{31}for he was teaching his disciples, saying to them, "The Child of Humanity will be betrayed and delivered into human hands. They will kill him, and the dead, after three days will rise."

^{32}The disciples did not understand this saying, but were afraid to question Jesus.

^{33}They arrived at Capernaum, and when they were in the house Jesus asked them, "What were you discussing on the way?"

^{34}But they were silent, for on the way they had argued with one another about who was the most important.

^{35}Sitting down, Jesus called the twelve and said to them, "If any one wants to be first, that one will be last of all and servant of all."

^{36}Then Jesus took a child and put it there in the midst of them, and holding the child in his arms, Jesus said to them, ^{37}"Whoever receives one such child in my name receives me, and whoever receives me receives not me but the one who sent me."

^{38}John said to him, "Teacher, we saw someone who does not follow us casting out demons in your name, and we stopped him, because he was not following us."

^{39}But Jesus said, "Do not forbid this, for no one who does a mighty work in my name can soon speak evil of me. ^{40}Whoever is not against us is for us. ^{41}Whoever gives you a cup of water to drink because you belong to Christ, truly I tell you, will never lose the reward.

^{42}"Whoever acts destructively against one of these little ones who believe in me, it would be better for that person to have a great millstone hung round the neck and be thrown into the sea. ^{43}If your hand is destructive, cut it off; it is better for you to enter life maimed than with two hands to go into gehenna*, to the unquench-able fire. ⁴⁵And if your foot is destructive, cut it off; it is better for you to enter life lame than with two feet to be thrown into gehen-na*. ⁴⁷And if your eye is destructive, pluck it out; it is better for you to enter the realm of God with one eye than with two eyes to be thrown into gehenna*. ⁴⁸'Where the worm does not die and the fire is not quenched.' *(Is 66:24)* ⁴⁹For everyone will be salted with fire. ⁵⁰Salt is good. But if salt becomes saltless, with what will you season it? Have salt in yourselves and be at peace with one an-other.''

Chapter X

¹AND LEAVING THERE, Jesus went to the region of Judea and across the Jordan, and again crowds went with him, and again, ac-cording to custom, he taught them.

²Pharisees came up and questioned Jesus, testing him, ''Is it lawful for a person to dismiss a spouse?''

³Jesus answered them, ''What did Moses command you?''

⁴They said, ''Moses allowed a person to dismiss a spouse by writing a certificate of divorce.''

⁵But Jesus said to them, ''Because of your hardness of heart Moses wrote you this commandment. ⁶But from the beginning of creation, God made them male and female. ⁷For this a person will leave father and mother and be joined to another, ⁸and the two shall become one. So they are no longer two but one flesh. ⁹What God has joined together, let not humans separate.''

¹⁰And in the house the disciples questioned Jesus further about this matter, ¹¹And Jesus said to them, ''A man who dismisses his wife and marries another commits adultery with her; ¹²and if a wo-man dismisses her husband and marries another, she commits adul-tery.''

¹³And people brought children to Jesus that he might touch them, but the disciples rebuked them. ¹⁴Seeing this Jesus was an-gry, and said to the disciples, ''Let the children come to me, do not hinder them. For God's dominion belongs to such as these. ¹⁵Truly I tell you, whoever does not accept the governance of God as a

*Gehenna, the valley of Hinnom, was the place outside the Jerusalem wall where waste and ritually unclean things were incinerated, the place of utmost abomination for Judeans.

child does shall never enter it.''

¹⁶And taking them in his arms, Jesus blessed the children, putting his hands on them.

¹⁷As Jesus went forth on his journey, someone ran up and knelt before him and asked, ''Good teacher, what must I do to inherit eternal life?''

¹⁸And Jesus replied, ''Why do you call me good? No one is good except one—God. ¹⁹You know the commandments, 'Do not kill, Do not commit adultery, Do not steal, Do not witness falsely, Do not defraud, Honor your father and mother.''' *(Ex 20.12-16)*

²⁰And the questioner said to Jesus, ''Teacher, all these I have observed since my youth.''

²¹But Jesus looking at the person lovingly said, ''You lack one thing. Go, sell what you have, and give to the poor, and you will have treasure in heaven. And come, follow me.''

²²At that saying the questioner was sad and, having many possessions, went away grieving.

²³Looking around, Jesus said to his disciples, ''How hard it will be for those who have riches to enter the realm of God!''

²⁴The disciples were amazed at these words. But Jesus said to them again, ''Children, how hard it is to enter the realm of God! ²⁵It is easier for a camel to go through the eye of a needle than for a rich person to enter the realm of God.''

²⁶The disciples were extremely astonished, and said among themselves, ''Then who can be saved?''

²⁷Looking at them Jesus said, ''With humans it is impossible, but not with God, for all things are possible with God.''

²⁸Peter began to say to Jesus, ''Look, we have left everything and followed you.''

²⁹Jesus said, ''Truly I tell you, there is no one who has left house or brothers or sisters or mother or father or children or lands, for my sake and for the gospel, ³⁰who will not receive a hundredfold now in this time, houses and brothers and sisters and mothers and children and lands, along with persecutions, and in the coming age eternal life. ³¹But many that are first will be last and the last first.''

³²They were all on the road going toward Jerusalem, with Je-

sus walking ahead of them, and the people were amazed, and those who followed were afraid.

Taking the twelve again, Jesus began to tell them what was to happen to him, ³³saying, "Look, we are going up to Jerusalem. There the Child of Humanity will be betrayed to the chief priests and the scribes, will be condemned to death, and delivered to the outsiders. ³⁴And they will mock and spit on him, and scourge and kill him. After three days Humanity's Child will rise again."

³⁵James and John, the two sons of Zebedee, approached Jesus and said, "Teacher, we want you to do for us what we ask of you."

³⁶Jesus said to them, "What do you want me to do for you?"

³⁷And they replied, "Allow us to sit, one at your right and one at your left, in your glory."

³⁸But Jesus said to them, "You do not know what you are asking. Can you drink the cup that I drink, or be baptized in the baptism I am baptized?"

³⁹And they replied, "We can."

And Jesus said to them, "The cup that I drink you will drink, and the baptism in which I am baptized, you will be baptized. ⁴⁰But to sit at my right or at my left is not mine to give, but is for those for whom it has been prepared."

⁴¹Hearing of these things, the ten became indignant at James and John. ⁴²And Jesus called them together and said, "You know that those who expect to rule over nations dictate to them, and their important people exercise authority over them. ⁴³But it shall not be so among you. Whoever wants to be important among you shall be your servant, ⁴⁴and whoever wants to be first among you shall be the slave of all. ⁴⁵For even Humanity's Child came not to be served but to serve, and to give this life as a ransom for many."

⁴⁶And they came to Jericho, and as Jesus was leaving Jericho along with his disciples and a large crowd, Bartimaeus, a blind beggar, the son of Timaeus, was sitting at the roadside. ⁴⁷And hearing that it was Jesus of Nazareth, Bartimaeus began to cry out and say, "Jesus, Child of David and Bathsheba, pity me!"

⁴⁸And many rebuked him, telling him to be quiet, but he cried out all the more, "Child of David and Bathsheba, pity me!"

⁴⁹Then Jesus standing there said, "Call him."

And people called to the blind man, saying, "Have courage. Get up, Jesus calls you." [50]So Bartimaeus threw off his garment, leaped up, and came to Jesus.

[51]And Jesus said to Bartimaeus, "What do you want me to do for you?"

And the blind man replied, "Rabboni, let me see again."

[52]Jesus said, "Go on your way, your faith has healed you." And immediately Bartimaeus saw again and followed Jesus on the road.

Chapter XI

[1]WHEN THEY DREW NEAR to Jerusalem, to Bethpage and Bethany, at the Mount of Olives, Jesus sent two of his disciples, [2]telling them, "Go into the village opposite you and as soon as you enter it you will find a colt tied, on which nobody has ever sat. Untie it and bring it. [3]If anyone says to you, 'Why are you doing this?' say, 'The Teacher needs it and will send it back here immediately.'"

[4]And they went and found a colt tied outside a door in the open street, and they untied it. [5]Some people standing there said to them, "What are you doing, untying the colt?"

[6]They told them what Jesus had said, and the people let the disciples go. [7]And they brought the colt to Jesus, and threw their garments on it, and he sat upon it. [8]Many other people spread their garments on the road, and others spread small branches which they had cut from the fields. [9]And those who went ahead and those who followed cried out, "Hosanna! (which means save) Blessed be the one who comes in the name of God! *(Ps 118.25, 26)* [10]Blessed be the coming nation of our ancestors David and Bathsheba! Hosanna in the highest!"

[11]Jesus entered Jerusalem, and went into the temple. When he had looked around at everything, it was already late, so he went back to Bethany with the twelve.

[12]On the following day, as they came from Bethany, Jesus was hungry. [13]And seeing in the distance a fig tree in leaf, he went to see if anything could be found on it. Coming to it, Jesus found nothing but leaves, for it was not the season for figs. [14]Jesus said

to the tree, "No one will ever eat your fruit again." And his disciples heard it.

¹⁵They arrived at Jerusalem, and Jesus entered the temple and began to drive out the buyers and the sellers from the temple. He overturned the tables of the money-changers and the seats of those who sold pigeons, ¹⁶and he would not allow anyone to carry any containers through the temple. ¹⁷Then Jesus taught them, saying, "Is it not written, 'My house shall be called a house of prayer for all the nations'? *(Is 56.7)* But you have made it a robbers' den." *(Jer 7:11)*

¹⁸And the chief priests and the scribes heard it and looked for a way to destroy Jesus, for they feared him because the whole crowd was amazed at his teaching. ¹⁹And when evening came Jesus and the disciples left the city.

²⁰As they passed by early in the morning, they saw the fig tree withered away to its roots. ²¹And Peter remembered and said to Jesus, "Rabbi, look! The fig tree which you cursed has withered."

²²And Jesus answering said to them, "Have faith in God. ²³Truly I tell you, whoever says to this mountain, 'Be picked up and thrown into the sea,' and has no inner doubts, but believes that whatever has been said will occur, that thing will be done for that person. ²⁴Therefore I tell you, whatever you request and ask for, believe that you have received it, and it will be done for you. ²⁵And whenever you stand praying, forgive, if you have anything against anyone, so that your God who is in heaven may also forgive you your trespasses."

²⁷So they arrived again at Jerusalem. As Jesus was walking in the temple, the chief priests and the scribes and the elders came to him, ²⁸and said, "By what authority are you doing these things, or who gave you this authority to do them?"

²⁹Jesus answered them, "I will question you and when you have answered me, I will tell you by what authority I do these things. ³⁰The baptism of John, was it heavenly or human? Answer me."

³¹And they debated among themselves saying, "If we say, 'From heaven,' Jesus will say, 'Why then did you not believe John?' ³²But can we say, 'From humans?'" They were afraid of

the crowd, for all the people held that John was really a prophet.

[33]So they answered Jesus, "We do not know."

And Jesus said to them, "Neither will I tell you by what authority I do these things."

Chapter XII

[1]AND JESUS BEGAN TO SPEAK to them in parables. "A person planted a vineyard, put a hedge around it, dug a wine press, built a tower, rented the vineyard to tenants, and then went away. [2]At the appropriate time the owner sent a slave to the tenants to get from them some of the fruit of the vineyard. [3]The tenants seized, beat, and sent the slave away with nothing. [4]Again the owner sent to them another slave, and that one they wounded in the head, and insulted. [5]And the owner sent another, and that one they killed. And so with many others, some they beat and some they killed. [6]The owner still had one other, a beloved child. Finally the owner sent this one to them, saying, 'They will respect my child.' [7]But those tenants said to one another, 'This is the heir; come, let us kill this one and the inheritance will be ours.' [8]So they seized and killed the child, and threw the body out of the vineyard. [9]What will the owner of the vineyard do? The owner will come and destroy the tenants, and give the vineyard to others. [10]Have you not read this scripture, 'The very stone which the builders rejected became the head of the corner; [11]this was God's doing, and it is marvelous in our eyes'?" *(Ps 118.22-23)*

[12]The authorities tried to arrest Jesus, but feared the crowds for they knew that Jesus had told the parable against them. So they left him and went away.

[13]Then they sent to Jesus some of the Pharisees and some of the Herodians, to entrap him with his own words. [14]These Pharisees and Herodians approached and said, "Teacher, we know that you are true, and are not intimidated by humans, for you do not regard the appearance of people but truly teach the way of God. Is it lawful to pay taxes to Caesar, or not? [15]Should we pay or should we not?"

But knowing their hypocrisy, Jesus said to them, "Why do you test me? Bring me a denarius and let me look at it."

^{16}They brought one, and Jesus asked them, "Whose portrait and inscription is this?"

They answered, "Caesar's."

^{17}Jesus said to them, "Pay to Caesar the things that are Caesar's, and to God the things that are God's." And they were amazed at him.

^{18}Then came Sadducees who say that there is no resurrection, and they questioned Jesus, ^{19}"Teacher, Moses wrote for us that if a man's brother dies and leaves a wife, but leaves no child, the brother must take the wife and raise up children for his brother. ^{20}Now there were seven brothers; the first took a wife, and died leaving no children; ^{21}and the second took her, and died leaving no children; and the third did the same; ^{22}and the seven left no children. Last of all the wife also died. ^{23}In the resurrection when they all rise again, to which husband will she be wife? For all seven had been husband to her."

^{24}Jesus said to them, "Do you not mistake because you know neither the scriptures nor the power of God? ^{25}For when the dead rise, they neither marry nor are given in marriage, but are like angels in heaven. ^{26}But about the dead being raised, have you not read in the book of Moses, in the part about the bush, how God said to him, 'I am the God of Abraham and Sarah, the God of Isaac and Rebecca, the God of Jacob, Leah and Rachel'? *(Ex 3.6)* ^{27}God is not for dead people, but for living. You are grossly mistaken."

^{28}Then one of the scribes came near and heard them debating, and knowing that Jesus answered them well, asked him, "What is the first commandment of all?"

^{29}Jesus answered, "The first is, 'Hear O Israel: Yahweh* our God is One God; ^{30}you shall love Yahweh your God with your whole heart, with your whole soul, with your whole mind, and with your whole strength.' *(Deut 6.4)* ^{31}The second is this, 'You shall love your neighbor as yourself.' *(Lev 19.18)* There is no other commandment greater than these."

^{32}The scribe said to Jesus, "Teacher, well and truly you say that God is one, and that there is no other but God, ^{33}and to love

---

*Yahweh = I am, or I am what I am, or perhaps: I am existence itself.
(Ex 3:14)

God with the whole heart, and the whole understanding, and the whole strength, and to love one's neighbor as oneself is more than all the burnt offerings and sacrifices."

[34]Then Jesus, seeing that the scribe answered wisely, said, "You are not far from the realm of God."

Then no one dared question Jesus any more.

[35]As Jesus taught in the temple, he said, "How can the scribes say that the Christ is the child of David and Bathsheba? [36]David himself, inspired by the Holy Spirit, declared, 'God said to my owner, sit at my right till I put your enemies under your feet.' *(Ps 110.1)* [37]If David himself calls this one 'owner,' how is this David's child?"

And the huge crowd heard Jesus gladly. [38]In his teaching, Jesus said, "Beware of the scribes, who like to go about in long robes and receive special greetings in the market places, [39]and have the chief seats in the synagogues and the places of honor at feasts, [40]who devour houses of widows and for a pretense make long prayers. These scribes will receive the greater condemnation."

[41]Sitting opposite the treasury, Jesus watched the crowd putting coins into the treasury, and many rich people put in large sums. [42]Then a poor widow came and put in two small coins, which make less than a penny. [43]And Jesus called together his disciples and said to them, "Truly I tell you, this poor widow has put in more than all the others who are putting money into the treasury. [44]For they all contributed out of their abundance, but she out of her poverty has put in everything she had, her whole living."

Chapter XIII

[1]AS JESUS CAME OUT of the temple, one of his disciples said to him, "Look, teacher, what great stones and what marvelous buildings!"

[2]And Jesus said to him, "Do you see these large buildings? There will not be left one stone upon another, that will not be thrown down."

[3]Then later when Jesus was sitting on the Mount of Olives opposite the temple, Peter and James and John and Andrew asked

him privately, [4]"Tell us, when will these things happen, and what will be the signal that these things are all about to be finished?"

[5]Jesus began by saying to them, "Take care that no one leads you astray. [6]For many will come in my name, saying, 'I am the one!' and they will lead many astray. [7]When you hear of wars and rumors of wars, do not be disturbed; this must happen, but the end is not yet. [8]For tribe will rise against tribe, and nation against nation; there will be earthquakes in some places; there will be famines; these things are the beginning of the birth pains.

[9]"But take care for yourselves, for they will deliver you up to councils, and you will be beaten in synagogues, and you will stand before leaders and rulers for my sake, to testify before them. [10]First the good news must be proclaimed to all nations. [11]While they lead you, bringing you to trial, do not be anxious beforehand about what you will say. Say whatever is given you at that moment, for it will not be you speaking, but the Holy Spirit.

[12]"And brother will deliver up brother to death, and parents will bring their children, and children will rise against parents and have them put to death. [13]And you will be hated by all for the sake of my name. But the one who endures to the end will be saved.

[14]"But when you see desolation's abomination *(Dan 11.31)* set up where it should not be (let the reader understand), then let those who are in Judea flee to the mountains. [15]Let not the one who is on the roof go down, nor enter the house to take anything away. [16]And let those in the field not go back to pick up their clothing or other possessions. [17]And alas for women who are pregnant and for those nursing a child in those days! [18]Pray that it may not happen in winter. [19]For in those days there will be such affliction as has not been from the beginning of creation which God created, until now, and never will be. [20]If God had not shortened the days, no human being would be saved, but for the sake of the chosen, whom God chose, the days are shortened.

[21]"Then if anyone tells you, 'Look, here is the Christ,' or 'Look, there!' do not believe it. [22]False christs and false prophets will arise and perform signs and wonders to deceive, if possible, the chosen ones. [23]But you see I have told you all things beforehand.

[24]"But in those days, after the affliction, the sun will be dark-

ened, and the moon will not give light, [25] and stars will be falling from heaven, and the powers of the heavens will be shaken. [26] And then they will see the Child of Humanity coming in clouds with great power and glory. [27] And then the Child will send the angels, and they will gather the chosen from the four winds, from the boundaries of the earth to the boundaries of heaven.

[28] "From the fig tree learn its lesson: when its branch becomes tender and puts forth leaves, you know that summer is near. [29] So also, when you see these things happening, you know that this is near, right at your doors. [30] Truly I tell you, this generation will not pass until all these things happen. [31] Heaven and earth will pass away but my words will not pass away.

[32] "But about that day and that hour no one knows, not the angels in heaven, nor Humanity's Child, but only God. [33] Watch, be awake, for you do not know when the time is. [34] It is like a person going on a journey, who when leaving home gives the slaves authority, each with work to do, and the doorkeeper's command is to be on the watch. [35] Watch, therefore, for you do not know when the head of the house will come, late in the day or at midnight, or at cockcrow, or early in the day. [36] If the arrival is sudden, you may be found asleep.

[37] "What I say to you I say to all: Watch."

Chapter XIV

[1] IT WAS NOW two days before the Passover and the Feast of Unleavened Bread. And the chief priests and the scribes were looking for a way to capture Jesus by trickery, to kill him. [2] For they said, "Not at the feast, lest the people riot."

[3] While Jesus was at Bethany in the house of Simon the leper, as he reclined at table, a woman came with an alabaster jar of ointment, pure nard, very costly; breaking the container, she poured the ointment over the head of Jesus. [4] Some there were angry and said among themselves "Why was this ointment wasted? [5] For this ointment might be sold for more than three hundred denarii, and given to the poor." And they were indignant with her.

[6] But Jesus said, "Leave her alone. Why do you cause her

trouble? She has done a good thing to me. ^{7}For you always have poor people with you, and whenever you wish, you can do them good, but you will not always have me. ^{8}She has done what she could; she has anointed my body beforehand for burial. ^{9}And truly I tell you, wherever the good news is proclaimed in the whole world, what she has done will be told as a memorial to her.''

^{10}Then Judas Iscariot, one of the twelve, went to the chief priests to betray Jesus to them. ^{11}And when they heard they rejoiced and promised to give Judas silver. And Judas sought an opportunity to betray Jesus.

^{12}On the first day of Unleavened Bread, when they sacrificed the Passover lamb, the disciples said to Jesus, ''Where do you want us to go to prepare the Passover for you to eat?''

^{13}Jesus sent two disciples, telling them, ''Go into the city, and a man carrying a jug of water will meet you; follow him, ^{14}and wherever he enters, say to the householder, 'The Teacher says, Where is my guest room where I may eat the passover with my disciples?' ^{15}And he will show you a large upper room furnished and ready. There prepare for us.''

^{16}So the disciples departed, went into the city, and found everything as Jesus had told them, and they prepared the passover.

^{17}When evening came Jesus arrived with the twelve. ^{18}And as they reclined and ate at the table, Jesus said, ''Truly I tell you, one of you will betray me, one who is eating with me.''

^{19}They began to grieve and to say to him one by one, ''Is it I?''

^{20}Jesus said to them, ''It is one of the twelve, one who is dipping in the same dish with me. ^{21}For the Child of Humanity must go as the writings declare, but woe to that person by whom Humanity's Child is betrayed! It would have been better for that person never to have been born.''

^{22}As they were eating, Jesus took bread, and blessed and broke it, and gave it to them, and said, ''Take this, it is my body.''

^{23}And he took a cup, and after giving thanks, gave it to them, and they all drank of it. ^{24}Jesus said, ''This is my blood of the new covenant, which is poured out for many. ^{25}Truly I tell you, I shall not drink again of the fruit of the vine until that day when I drink it new in the realm of God.''

²⁶After singing a hymn, they went out to the Mount of Olives. ²⁷And Jesus said to them, "You will all be driven away, for it is written, 'I will strike the shepherd, and the sheep will be scattered.' *(Zech 13.7)* ²⁸But after I am raised up, I will go ahead of you to Galilee."

²⁹Peter said, "Even though they all are driven away, I will not."

³⁰And Jesus said to Peter, "Truly I tell you, today, this very night, before the cock crows twice, you will deny me three times."

³¹But Peter said more vehemently, "If I must die with you, I will not deny you." And all said the same.

³²They came to a part of the hillside which was called Gethsemane, and Jesus said to his disciples, "Sit here while I pray." ³³Then he took Peter, James, and John along with him and began to be greatly agitated and distressed. ³⁴And he said to them, "My soul is deeply grieved, even to death; stay here and watch."

³⁵And going a little farther, Jesus fell on the ground and prayed that, if it were possible, the time might pass from him. ³⁶And he said, "Holy source of my being, all things are possible to you; remove this cup from me. Yet, not what I desire, but what you will."

³⁷Jesus came back, found the others sleeping, and said to Peter, "Simon, are you asleep? Could you not watch one hour? ³⁸Watch and pray that you may not enter into temptation. Indeed the spirit is eager, but the flesh is weak."

³⁹And again leaving them, Jesus prayed, saying the same words. ⁴⁰And returning found them sleeping, for their eyes were very heavy. They did not know what to answer him.

⁴¹Jesus came a third time, and said to them, "Do you sleep and take your rest? It is enough. The time has come. Look, Humanity's Child is betrayed into the hands of sinners. ⁴²Stand up, let us be going. See, my betrayer is here."

⁴³And immediately, while Jesus was still speaking, Judas, one of the twelve, arrived with a crowd from the chief priests and the scribes and the elders; many carried swords and clubs. ⁴⁴Now the betrayer had given them a signal, saying, "Whomever I shall kiss is the one; seize him and lead him away well secured."

⁴⁵Immediately on arrival, Judas went up to Jesus and said,

"Rabbi!" and fervently kissed him.

46Then they laid hands on Jesus and captured him. 47But one of those who stood by drew a sword and struck a slave of the high priest and cut off his ear. 48And Jesus said to them, "Have you come out as against a robber, with swords and clubs to arrest me? 49Day after day I was with you teaching in the temple and you did not seize me. But let the scriptures be fulfilled."

50And the disciples all left him and fled. 51A certain young man who accompanied Jesus was wearing nothing but a light garment on his body when they seized him, 52and he left the garment and ran away naked.

53Then they led Jesus to the high priest, and all the chief priests, elders, and scribes were assembled.

54Peter followed Jesus at a distance, and came into the courtyard of the high priest and sat with the attendants, warming himself by the fire.

55Now the chief priests and the whole council sought testimony against Jesus to put him to death, but they found none. 56For many falsely witnessed against him, but their testimonies did not agree. 57Some stood up and falsely witnessed against Jesus, saying, 58"We heard him say, 'I will destroy this temple that is made with hands, and in three days I will build another, not made with hands.'" 59Yet even so their testimonies did not agree.

60Then the high priest stood up in their midst, and questioned Jesus, "Have you no answer to what these people testify against you?"

61But Jesus was silent and answered nothing.

Again the high priest questioned him, "Are you the Christ, the child of the Blessed One?"

62Then Jesus said, "I am. And you will see Humanity's Child sitting at the right hand of power, and coming with the clouds of heaven."

63At this the high priest tore his tunics and said, "What need have we of witnesses? 64You have heard the blasphemy. What is your decision?"

They all condemned Jesus as deserving death. 65And some began to spit on him, and covered his face, and struck him, saying

"Prophesy!" And the attendants, striking Jesus, took him away.

66As Peter was below in the courtyard, one of the maidservants of the high priest came 67and saw Peter warming himself. Looking at him, she said, "You also were with this Nazarene, Jesus."

68Peter denied it, saying, "I neither know nor understand what you say." And he went outside into the forecourt.

69The maidservant saw him, and began again to say to the bystanders, "This man is one of them."

70But again Peter denied it. After a little while again the bystanders said to Peter, "Certainly you are one of them, for you are a Galilean."

71Then Peter began to curse and swear, "I do not know this person of whom you speak."

72And immediately a cock crowed a second time. Then Peter remembered that Jesus had said to him, "Before the cock crows twice, you will deny me three times." Thinking of this, Peter wept.

Chapter XV

1AS SOON AS it was morning the chief priests, the elders and scribes, and the whole Sanhedrin held a council, then they bound Jesus, led him away and delivered him to Pilate.

2Pilate questioned Jesus, "You are Ruler of the Judeans?" Jesus answered, "You have said so."

3The chief priests accused Jesus of many things. 4Then Pilate questioned him again, "Have you no answer to make? See how many accusations they make against you."

5But Jesus answered nothing more, so that Pilate was amazed.

6Now at the feast Pilate would release for the people a prisoner for whom they asked. 7Among the rebels bound in prison, who had done murder during the rebellion, there was one called Barabbas. 8And the crowd approached and began to ask Pilate to do as usual for them. 9And Pilate answered them, "Do you want me to release for you the Ruler of the Judeans?" 10For Pilate perceived that it was out of envy that the chief priests had delivered Jesus up. 11But the chief priests stirred up the crowd to have Pilate release Barabbas to them instead.

¹²Pilate again said to them, "Then what shall I do with the one whom you call the Ruler of the Judeans?"

¹³The crowd shouted, "Crucify him."

¹⁴Pilate said, "Why, what evil has he done?"

But they cried out all the more, "Crucify!"

¹⁵Pilate decided to satisfy the crowd, and released Barrabas to them. Then, having scourged him, Pilate delivered Jesus to be crucified.

¹⁶The soldiers led Jesus away into the palace (that is the praetorium), and there called together the whole cohort. ¹⁷They put a purple robe on Jesus, and plaited a thorny crown for his head. ¹⁸They began to salute Jesus, "Hail, Ruler of the Judeans!" ¹⁹They struck his head with a reed; they spat upon him; they knelt to worship him. ²⁰When they had mocked him, they removed the purple robe, put his own clothes on him, and led Jesus out to be crucified.

²¹They compelled a passerby named Simon, a Cyrenian, coming in from the country, and the father of Alexander and Rufus, to carry the cross of Jesus. ²²They brought him to the place called Golgotha (which means place of the skull). ²³They offered Jesus wine spiced with myrrh, but he did not take it. ²⁴They crucified Jesus, and divided his garments by casting lots for them to decide what each should take.

²⁵Now it was the third hour when they crucified Jesus. ²⁶And the inscription of his accusation was written, "The Ruler of the Judeans." ²⁷With Jesus they crucified two robbers, one on his right and one on his left. ²⁸And the scripture was fulfilled which says, "He was counted among the transgressors." *(Is 53.12)* ²⁹Those passing by derided Jesus, wagging their heads and saying, "Aha! You who would destroy the temple and build it in three days, ³⁰save yourself. Come down from the cross!"

³¹In like manner the chief priests also mocked Jesus to one another with the scribes, saying, "He saved others, but cannot save himself. ³²Let this Christ, this Ruler of Israel, come down now from the cross, that we may see and believe."

Those who were crucified with Jesus also reviled him.

³³At the sixth hour, darkness came over the whole land, until

the ninth hour. [34]At the ninth hour Jesus cried with a loud voice, "Eloi, Eloi, Lama sabachthani?" which means, "My God, my God, why have you forsaken me?"

[35]Some of the bystanders hearing it said, "Listen, he is calling Elijah."

[36]Some ran and filled a sponge with vinegar, placed it on a reed and gave it to Jesus to drink, saying, "Wait, let us see whether Elijah will come to take him down."

[37]But Jesus, with a loud cry, breathed his last. [38]The curtain of the temple was torn in two, from top to bottom. [39]When the centurion standing by in front of him saw that Jesus thus expired, he said, "Surely this was a child of God!"

[40]There were also women watching from afar, among whom were both Mary Magdalene and Mary the mother of James the younger and of Joses, and Salome [41]who, when Jesus was in Galilee, had followed and served him, and also many others who came up with him to Jerusalem.

[42]When it was evening, since it was the day of Preparation, which is the day before the sabbath, [43]Joseph of Arimathea, an honorable member of the council, who was also himself expecting the reign of God, taking courage, went to Pilate and asked for the body of Jesus. [44]Pilate was amazed that Jesus was already dead, and summoning the centurion, questioned whether he had already died. [45]When Pilate had ascertained this from the centurion, he granted the body to Joseph. [46]Having bought a piece of new linen, and taking Jesus down, Joseph wrapped the body in the linen, placed it in a tomb which had been hewn out of rock, and rolled a stone against the door of the tomb. [47]Mary Magdalene and Mary the mother of Joses saw where the body of Jesus was placed.

Chapter XVI

[1]WHEN THE SABBATH was past, Mary Magdalene, Mary the mother of James, and Salome, bought spices that they might go and anoint the body of Jesus. [2]Very early on the first day of the week they arrived at the tomb as the sun was rising. [3]They were saying to one another, "Who will roll away the stone for us from

the door of the tomb?"

⁴Looking up, they saw that the stone was already rolled back. It was very large. ⁵Entering the tomb, they saw a young man sitting on the right side, dressed in a white robe, and they were amazed. ⁶But he said to them, "Do not be amazed. You seek Jesus of Nazareth who was crucified. Jesus has risen and is not here. See the place where they put the body. ⁷But go, tell the disciples and Peter that Jesus is going before you to Galilee, and will meet you there as he told you."

⁸The women reported briefly to Peter and those with him all that they had been told. And after this, Jesus sent forth by means of them, from east to west, the sacred and imperishable proclamation of eternal salvation.

Alternative to Chapter XVI

Now when Jesus rose early on the first day of the week, and appeared first to Mary Magdalene, from whom had been cast out seven demons, she went and told those who had been with Jesus, as they mourned and wept. Hearing that Jesus was alive and had been seen by her, they did not believe it.

After this Jesus appeared in different form to two of them as they walked in the country. Those two went back and told the rest but they did not believe them either.

Still later Jesus appeared to the eleven as they reclined at table, and reproached their unbelief and hardness of heart, because they had not believed those who witnessed that Jesus was risen.

Jesus said to them, "Go into all the world and proclaim the good news to the whole creation, Any one who believes and is baptized will be saved, but those who do not believe will be condemned. And these signs will accompany those who believe: in my name they will cast out demons; they will speak in new tongues; they will pick up serpents, and if they drink any deadly thing, it will not hurt them; and when they place their hands on the sick, the sick will recover."

Then Jesus, after speaking to them, was taken up into heaven, and sat with God. But the disciples went forth and proclaimed the word everywhere, while God worked with them and confirmed their message by the signs that attended it. *Amen.*

The Epistle to the Romans

Chapter I

[1]PAUL, A SLAVE of Christ Jesus, called to be an apostle, set apart for God's good news, [2]which God had promised earlier through the prophets in the holy scriptures [3]concerning the Child of God, who was descended from David and Bathsheba according to the flesh, [4]and designated Child of God in power according to the spirit of holiness by resurrection of the dead, Jesus Christ whom we serve, [5]through whom we receive grace and apostleship to bring about obedience by faith among all the nations on behalf of the name of Jesus, [6]among whom you also are called to belong to Jesus Christ:

[7]To all God's beloved in Rome, who are called holy:

Grace to you and peace from God our Creator and Jesus Christ whom we serve.

[8]First, I thank my God through Jesus Christ for all of you, because your faith is proclaimed throughout the world. [9]For God, whom I serve in my spirit in the good news of God's Child, is my witness that without ceasing I mention you always in my prayers, [10]asking that somehow by God's will I may sometime make the happy journey and come to you. [11]For I long to see you, that I may impart to you some spiritual gift for your foundation, [12]and that we may encourage one another's faith, both yours and mine.

[13]But I want you to know, brothers and sisters, that though prevented thus far, I have often intended to come to you, that I may reap some harvest among you as well as among the rest of the nations. [14]I am a debtor both to Greeks and to foreigners, both to the wise and to the foolish; [15]insofar as is in my power, I am eager to proclaim the good news also to you who are in Rome.

[16]For I am not ashamed of the good news. It is the power of God for salvation to everyone who believes it, to the Judean first, but also to the Greek. [17]For the righteousness of God is revealed in

it from faith to faith, as it is written, "The just person shall live by faith." *(Hab 2.4)*

[18] For the wrath of God is revealed from heaven against all ungodliness and unrighteousness of people who by their wickedness suppress the truth. [19]For what is known of God is visible to them, because God has shown it to them. [20]From the creation of the world God's invisible qualities, namely, eternal power and divinity, have been understood and clearly seen in the things that have been made. So they are without excuse, [21]for although they knew God they did not give glory or give thanks to God, but they became futile in their reasoning and their undiscerning minds were darkened. [22]Claiming to be wise, they became foolish, [23]and exchanged the glory of the immortal God for images of mortal humans, birds, animals, and reptiles.

[24]Therefore God gave them up in the lusts of their hearts to uncleanness, to the dishonoring of their bodies among themselves, [25]because they exchanged God's truth for a lie, and worshiped and served created things rather than the Creator, who is blessed for ever! *Amen.*

[26]Therefore, God gave them up to dishonorable passions. Even the females exchanged natural relations for unnatural, [27]and the males likewise gave up natural relations with females and burned with desire for one another, males doing unseemly acts with males and receiving back in their own persons the necessary repayment for their error.

[28]And since they did not see fit to acknowledge God, God gave them up to a base mind and to improper conduct. [29]They were filled with all kinds of unrighteousness, wickedness, covetousness, evil. Full of envy, murder, strife, deceit, malignity, they are gossips, [30]slanderers, haters of God, insolent, arrogant, boastful, inventors of evil, disobedient to parents, [31]foolish, faithless, heartless, and unmerciful. [32]Although they know God's decree that those who practice such things deserve to die, they not only do them but approve others who practice them.

Chapter II

[1]THEREFORE YOU PEOPLE have no excuse when you judge others, for in whatever you judge others you condemn yourself, because you are doing the very same things. [2]We know that the judgment of God is according to truth upon those who do such things. [3]Do you people suppose that when you judge those who do such things while doing them yourselves, you will escape the judgment of God? [4]Or do you despise the riches of God's kindness, forbearance, and patience, not knowing that God's kindness leads you to repentance? [5]But by your hard and impenitent hearts you are storing up wrath for yourselves, on the day of wrath and revelation of God's righteous judgment. [6]For God will repay each person according to his or her works. [7]To those who by patient good works seek glory, honor, and immortality, God will give eternal life. [8]But for those who are self-seeking and obey wickedness rather than obey the truth, there will be wrath and anger. [9]There will be affliction and anguish for every human soul who works evil, the Judean first but also the Greek. [10]But there will be glory and honor and peace for everyone who does good, the Judean first, but also the Greek. [11]For God shows no partiality.

[12]All who have sinned without the law will also perish without the law, and all who have sinned under the law will be judged by the law. [13]For it is not hearers of the law who are righteous before God, but doers of the law will be justified. [14]For whenever people who do not have the law do by nature what the law requires, they are a law to themselves, even though they do not have the law. [15]They show that what the law requires is written in their hearts, while their conscience also witnesses, and their exchanges of thoughts with one another accuse or excuse one another, [16]on that day when according to my gospel, God judges the secrets of people through Christ Jesus.

[17]But if you call yourself a Judean and rely upon the law and boast in God [18]and know God's will and approve what is excellent, because you are instructed in the law, [19]and having persuaded yourself that you are a guide to the blind, a light to those in darkness, [20]an instructor of the foolish, a teacher of little children, hav-

ing in the law the form of knowledge and truth, [21]you then who teach others, will you not teach yourself? While you tell others not to steal, do you steal? [22]You that tell others not to commit adultery, do you commit adultery? You that abhor idols, do you rob temples? [23]You that boast in the law, do you dishonor God by breaking the law? [24]For as it is written, "The name of God is blasphemed among the nations because of you." *(Is 52.5/Ezek 36.22)*

[25]The formal covenant is of value only if you obey the law; but if you break the law, your covenant becomes unratified. [26]So, if people who are not in the legal community keep the precepts of the law, will not their extra-legal acts be regarded as legality? [27]Then those who are not initiated into the legal covenant, but keep the law, will condemn you who have the written law and covenant but break the law. [28]For that person is not a real Judean who is one only outwardly, nor is true covenant something external and physical. [29]Being a Judean is an inward state, for real covenant is a matter of the heart, in spirit rather than in letter, and its praise is not from people but from God.

Chapter III

[1]THEN WHAT ADVANTAGE have Judeans? Or what is the value of their legal covenant? [2]Much in every way. First because the Judeans were entrusted with the oracles of God. [3]For what? If some disbelieved, does their unbelief destroy God's faithfulness? [4]Impossible! Let God be true though every person be false, as it is written, "That you may be justified in your words, and will overcome when you are judged." *(Ps 51.4)* [5]But if our unrighteousness serves to show God's righteousness, what shall we say? That God is unjust to inflict wrath on us? (I speak in a human way.) [6]Impossible! For then how could God judge the world? [7]But if through my lie God's truth abounds to God's glory, why am I still judged as a sinner? [8]And why not—as some people slanderously charge us with saying—"Do evil that good may come?" Their condemnation is just.

[9]What then? Do we excel? Not at all. For we have already charged that all people, both Judeans and Greeks, are under the

power of sin. [10]As it is written: "There is not one righteous person, not one. [11]There is not one who understands, nor one who seeks God. [12]All have turned away; together they have gone wrong; no one does kindness, not even one." *(Ps 14.1-3/Ps 53.1-3/ Eccles 7.20)* [13]"Their throat is an open grave, they use their tongues to deceive." *(Ps 5.9)* "The venom of asps is under their lips." *(Ps 140.3)* [14]"Their mouth is full of curses and bitterness." *(Ps 10.7)* [15]"Their feet are swift to shed blood; [16]in their ways are ruin and misery; [17]and they do not know the way of peace." *(Is 59.7-8)* [18]"There is no fear of God before their eyes." *(Ps 36.1)*

[19]Now we know that whatever the law says it speaks to those who are under the law, so that every mouth may be silenced, and the whole world may be held under judgment of God. [20]For no human being will be justified before God by works of law since through law comes full knowledge of sin.

[21]But now God's righteousness has been shown apart from law, although both law and the prophets witness to it. [22]It is righteousness of God through faith in Jesus Christ for all who believe. There are no distinctions, [23]for all have sinned and fallen short of the glory of God. [24]All are justified freely by God's grace, through redemption in Christ Jesus, [25]whom God put forward as a propitiation by Christ's blood, through faith. This was to show God's righteousness, because in overlooking former sins, [26]God's forbearance and righteousness at the present time show God to be just and justifying those who have faith in Jesus.

[27]What then becomes of boasting? It is excluded. On what law? The law of works? No, but through the rule of faith. [28]For we count a person justified by faith, outside of works of law. [29]Or is God the God of Judeans only? Is God not the God of outsiders also? Yes, of others as well, [30]since there is one God who will justify the community under law by their faith, and the community outside the law by their faith. [31]Do we then destroy the law by this faith? Not at all! Rather, we uphold the law.

Chapter IV

[1]THEN WHAT SHALL WE SAY that our human ancestors,

Abraham and Sarah, discovered? [2]For if Abraham and Sarah were justified by works, they have something to boast about, but not before God. [3]For what does the scripture say? "Abraham and Sarah trusted God, and it was counted as righteousness for them." *(Gen 15.6)* [4]Now to the working person wages are not counted as a gift but as a debt owed. [5]And to one not working, but trusting someone who justifies the ungodly, his or her faith is counted as righteousness. [6]So also David declares the blessedness of the person to whom God counts righteousness outside of works, [7]"Blessed are those whose lawlessness is forgiven, and whose sins are covered, [8]blessed is the one against whom God will not count sin." *(Ps 32.1-2)*

[9]Is this blessing pronounced only upon the legal community, or also upon outsiders? We say that faith was counted for Sarah and Abraham as righteousness. [10]How then was it counted for them? Was it before or after they entered the covenant? It was not after, but before, while they were still outsiders. [11]They received the sign or seal of their righteousness which they held by faith while they were still without the covenant. The purpose was to make Sarah and Abraham parents of all who believe without being in the legal community and who thus have righteousness counted for them, [12]and likewise they are parents of the legal community who are not merely lawful but also follow the example of the faith which our ancestors Abraham and Sarah had prior to the covenant.

[13]The promise to Sarah and Abraham and their descendants, that they should inherit the world, did not come through the law but through the righteousness of faith. [14]If it is through law that this inheritance comes, then faith is empty and the promise destroyed. [15]For the law brings wrath, but where there is no law there is no transgression.

[16]Therefore, it depends on faith, that by grace the promise may be guaranteed to all descendants—not only to descendants of the law but also to the descendants of the faith of Abraham and Sarah, for they are the parents of us all. [17]As it is written, "I have made you the parents of many nations," *(Gen 17.5)* in the presence of God in whom they believed, who gives life to the dead and calls into being things that are not. [18]In hope they believed against hope,

that they should become the parents of many nations, as they had been told, "So shall your descendants be." *(Gen 15.5)* [19]They did not weaken in faith when they considered their own bodies, which were as good as dead because they were nearly a hundred years old, or when they considered the barrenness of Sarah's womb. [20]They did not falter through unbelief in the promise of God, but were empowered by their faith, giving glory to God, [21]fully persuaded that God was able to fulfill the promise. [22]That is why their faith was "counted to them as righteousness." [23]But the words, "It was counted to them," were written not for them alone, [24]but for us also. For it will be counted as righteousness to believers in the God who raised from the dead Jesus Christ, [25]who was put to death for our offenses and raised for our justification.

Chapter V

[1]THEREFORE, since we are justified by faith, we have peace with God through Jesus Christ whom we serve. [2]Through Christ we also have access by faith to this grace in which we stand, and we claim the hope of God's glory. [3]More than that, we accept affliction proudly, knowing that affliction produces patience, [4]and patience produces proof, and proof produces hope, [5]and hope does not shame us, because God's love has been poured into our hearts through the Holy Spirit which has been given to us.

[6]While we were yet powerless and weak, at the right time Christ died for the ungodly. [7]But one will hardly die for a righteous person, though perhaps for a good person one will dare even to die, [8]but God shows love for us in that Christ died for us while we were still sinners. [9]Since, therefore, we are now justified by Christ's blood, much more shall we be saved through Christ from the wrath of God. [10]For if while we were yet enemies we were reconciled to God through the death of the Child of God, how much more, now that we are reconciled shall we be saved by the life of Christ. [11]Not only so, but we also boast in God through Jesus Christ whom we serve, through whom we have now received reconciliation.

[12]Therefore, as sin came into the world through one incident, and through sin came death, so death came to all people since all

people sinned. [13]Sin indeed was in the world before law, but sin is not counted when there is no law. [14]Yet death reigned from Adam and Eve until Moses and Miriam, even over those whose sins were not like the transgression of Adam and Eve, who were prototypes of the one who was to come.

[15]But the free gift is not like evil action. For if many died through one offense, much more have God's grace, and the gift in the grace of that one person Jesus Christ, abounded for many. [16]And the gift is not like the effect of that one offense, for the judgment after one offense led to condemnation, but the free gift after many offenses led to justification. [17]For if by one offense death reigned through that one, much more will life reign in those who receive the abundance of grace and the gift of righteousness through the one Jesus Christ.

[18]So therefore, as through one offense came condemnation for all people, so also through one righteous act came the justification of life to all people. [19]For as by one person's disobedience many were made sinners, so also by one person's obedience many will be made righteous. [20]Law came in so that offenses might abound, but where sin abounded, grace abounded all the more. [21]Thus, as sin reigned by death, so also grace could reign through righteousness toward eternal life through Jesus Christ whom we serve.

Chapter VI

[1]WHAT SHALL WE SAY then? Do we continue in sin so that grace may abound? [2]Not at all! If we died to sin, how can we live in it? [3]Or do you not know that all of us who have been baptized into Christ Jesus were immersed in the death of Christ Jesus. [4]Therefore, we were buried with Jesus by immersion into death, so that, as Christ was raised from the dead through the glory of God, we also might walk in new life.

[5]For if we have been united with Jesus in the same death, we shall certainly be united in the same resurrection. [6]We know that our old self was crucified with Jesus to destroy bodily sin, so that we no longer are enslaved to sin. [7]For one who has died is released from sin. [8]But if we died with Jesus, we believe that we also live

with Christ. [9]For we know that Christ, raised from the dead, never dies again; death no longer rules over Christ. [10]In dying, Jesus died once to sin, but in living, lives to God. [11]So you also consider yourselves dead to sin, but living to God in Christ Jesus.

[12]Therefore, let not sin rule your mortal body, to make you obey its lusts. [13]Do not offer parts of your body to sin as weapons of unrighteousness, but offer yourselves to God as a person once dead, now living, and the parts of your body to God as weapons of righteousness. [14]For sin will not rule over you, because you are not under law but are under grace.

[15]What then? May we sin because we are not under law but under grace? Not at all! [16]Do you not know that to whomever you offer yourselves as obedient slaves, you are slaves of the one you obey, whether of sin leading to death, or of obedience leading to righteousness? [17]But thanks to God, you that were slaves of sin have obeyed from the heart a form of teaching to which you were brought, [18]and, having been freed from sin, have become slaves of righteousness. [19]I am speaking in human terms, because of your human weaknesses. For as you offered your bodily parts as slaves to impurity, from iniquity to iniquity, so now offer your bodily parts to righteousness for sanctification.

[20]When you were slaves of sin, you were free of righteousness. [21]What return did you then receive from the things of which you are now ashamed? The end of those things is death. [22]But now that you have been freed from sin and have become slaves of God, the return you get is sanctification and its end, eternal life. [23]For the compensation for sin is death, but the free gift of God is eternal life in Christ Jesus whom we serve.

Chapter VII

[1]DO YOU NOT KNOW, sisters and brothers—for I am speaking to those who know the law—that the law is binding on people only while they live? [2]Thus a married person is bound by law to the spouse as long as they both live, but if one spouse dies the other is discharged from the law concerning the dead spouse. [3]Accordingly, one will be called an adulterer if one lives with a different person

while the first spouse is alive. But if one spouse dies the other is free from that law, and may marry another without being called an adulterer.

[4]Similarly, my sisters and brothers, through the body of Christ you have died in relation to the law, so that you may belong to another, to the one who has been raised from the dead in order that we may bear fruit for God. [5]While we were living in the flesh, sin's passions operated through the law in our bodily parts to bear fruit for death. [6]But now we are discharged from the law, dead to that which held us captive, so that we do not serve the old written code but the new Spirit.

[7]What then shall we say? That the law is sin? Not at all! Yet I knew sin only through law. I would not know about lust if the law had not said, "You shall not lust." [8]But sin, finding opportunity through the commandment, produced in me all kinds of lust. Without law sin is dead. [9]I once lived without law, but when the commandment came, sin came alive [10]and I died. This commandment which promised life was for death. [11]For sin, finding opportunity through the commandment, deceived me and through the commandment killed me. [12]So the law is holy, and the commandment is holy, just, and good.

[13]Did the good, then, bring me death? Not at all! but sin produced death in me through the good, to cause sin to be recognized as sin, and so that through the commandment sin might be shown to be totally sinful. [14]We know that the law is spiritual, but I am carnal, sold under sin. [15]I do not understand my own actions. For I do not practice what I wish, but I do the very thing I hate. [16]Now if I do that which I do not wish to do, I agree that the law is good. [17]So then it is no longer I that do it, but the sin which resides within me. [18]For I know that nothing good lives within me, that is, in my flesh. I can wish for the good, but I cannot do it. [19]For I do not do the good I intend, but I practice the evil that I do not want. [20]Now if I do what I do not want, it is no longer I that cause it to be done, but the sin residing in me.

[21]So I find it to be a law that when I am wishing to do good, evil is present in me. [22]For I delight in the law of God in my inmost self, [23]but I see in my bodily parts a different law warring against

the law of my mind and making me captive by the law of sin residing in my bodily parts. [24]Wretched person that I am! Who will deliver me from this body of death? [25]Thanks be to God through Jesus Christ whom we serve! So then, I of myself serve the law of God with my mind, but with my flesh I serve the law of sin.

Chapter VIII

[1]THERE IS, THEREFORE, now no condemnation for those who are in Christ Jesus. [2]For the law of the spirit of life in Christ Jesus has freed us from the law of sin and death. [3]That which was impossible under the law weakened by human nature, God accomplished by sending the Child of God in the likeness of sinful flesh; and concerning sin, God condemned the sin residing in the flesh, [4]in order that the justice of the law might be fulfilled in us who walk not according to the flesh but according to the spirit.

[5]Those who live according to the flesh set their minds on the things of the flesh, but those who live according to the spirit set their minds on the things of the spirit. [6]Setting the mind on the flesh leads to death, but setting the mind on the spirit is life and peace. [7]For the mind concentrated on the flesh is hostile to God. It does not submit to God's law, indeed it cannot. [8]And those who are in the flesh cannot please God.

[9]You are not in the flesh, but are in the spirit, since the spirit of God resides within you. But any one who does not have the spirit of Christ does not belong to Christ. [10]But if Christ is in you, although your bodies are dead because of sin, your spirits are alive because of righteousness. [11]If the spirit of the one who raised Christ from the dead resides in you, then the one who raised Christ from the dead will give life also to your mortal bodies through God's spirit residing within you.

[12]So then, brothers and sisters, we are not debtors to the flesh, nor living according to the flesh. [13]For living according to the flesh leads to death, but if by the spirit you kill the actions belonging to the body, you will live. [14]All who are led by the spirit of God are children of God. [15]For you did not receive the spirit of slavery to return into fear, but you have received the spirit of adoption, by

which you cry, "God, I am your child!" [16]It is, in fact, the spirit witnessing with our spirits that we are children of God. [17]And if children, then heirs; heirs of God as well as joint heirs with Christ; suffering with Christ in order that we also may be glorified with Christ.

[18]I consider that the sufferings of this present time are not worth comparing with the coming glory that will be revealed to us. [19]For creation, anxious, eager, and watchful, longs for the revealing of God's children. [20]Creation was ruled by futility not willingly but by the will of the one who enslaved it; in hope, [21]because the creation itself will be set free from slavery to decay, set free for the glory of the children of God. [22]We know that the whole creation has been groaning and laboring together until now, [23]and not only creation, but we ourselves, who have the first fruits of the spirit, groan inwardly as we anticipate adoption as sons and daughters, the redemption of our bodies.

[24]We were saved by hope. But hope that is seen is not hope. For why hope for what is already seen? [25]But if we hope for what we do not see, we anticipate it with patience. [26]Similarly the spirit shares in our weakness. And as we pray for what we cannot understand, the spirit itself intercedes for us with groans that have no voice. [27]And the One who searches all hearts knows the mind of the spirit, because the spirit intercedes for the saints in accordance with God's will.

[28]With those who love God and are called in accordance with God's purpose, we know that God causes all things to work together for good. [29]Those whom God foreknew and predestined are conformed to the image of the Child of God, so that Jesus would be the first-born among many sisters and brothers. [30]And those who were predestined God also called, and those who were called God also justified, and those who were justified God also glorified.

[31]What then shall we say to this? If God acts on our behalf, who can stand against us? [32]Not sparing God's own child, but delivering Jesus up for us all, will not God, with Jesus, also freely give all things to us? [33]Who could bring any charge against the chosen ones of God? If God justifies, [34]who could condemn? Christ Jesus

died, but since being raised from the dead, is at the hand of God, and now intercedes for us? [35]Who will separate us from the love of Christ? Shall tribulation, or distress, or persecution, or famine, or nakedness, or peril, or sword? [36]As it is written, "For your sake we are being killed all day long; we are regarded as sheep to be slaughtered." *(Ps 44.22)* [37]No, in all these things we are more than conquerors through the one who loved us. [38]For I am persuaded that neither death, nor life, nor angels, nor rulers, nor things present nor things to come, nor powers, [39]nor height, nor depth, nor any other creature, will be able to separate us from the love of God in Christ Jesus whom we serve.

Chapter IX

[1]I SPEAK THE TRUTH in Christ, I do not lie. My conscience witnesses with me in the Holy Spirit, [2]that I have great sorrow and unceasing pain in my heart. [3]For I have prayed that I myself were accursed and cut off from Christ for the sake of my sisters and brothers, who are my kin according to flesh. [4]They are Israelites, and to them belong the adoption, the glory, the covenants, the giving of the law, the worship, and the promises. [5]Theirs are our ancestors, and of their lineage, according to the flesh, is the Christ, the one God blessed above all for ever. *Amen.*

[6]Not of course, that God's word has failed, for not all from Israel belong to Israel. [7]Not all who are descendants of Sarah and Abraham are their true children, but, "Through Isaac and Rebecca shall your descendants be called." *(Gen 21.12)* [8]Meaning that it is not merely children of the flesh who are Children of God, but the children of the promise are counted as descendants. [9]For this is what the promise said, "About this time I will return and Sarah shall bear a son." *(Gen 18.10)* [10]And not only so, but also when Rebecca had conceived by Isaac our ancestor, [11]before the children were born and before they had done anything either good or bad, in order that God's purpose according to choice might continue, [12]not because of works but because of God's call, Rebecca was told, "The elder will serve the younger." *(Gen 25.23)* [13]As it is written, "Jacob I loved, but Esau I hated." *(Mal 1.2-3)*

[14]What shall we say then? Is there no justice with God? Not at all! [15]For God says to Moses, "I will have mercy on whomever I have mercy, and I will pity whomever I pity." *(Ex 33.19)* [16]So nothing happens by wishing nor by exertion, but by God's mercy. [17]For the scripture says to Pharaoh, "I have raised you up for the very purpose of showing my power in you, so that my name may be proclaimed abroad throughout all the earth." *(Ex 9.16)* [18]Therefore, God chooses on whom to have mercy, and whose heart is to be hardened.

[19]You will say to me then, "Why does God still find fault? For who can resist the determination of God?" [20]But you are a human being; how dare you answer back to God? Will the thing formed say to the one who formed it, "Why have you made me like this?" [21]Has not the potter authority over the clay, to make out of the same lump one superior vessel and another inferior? [22]But wishing to demonstrate wrath and power, what if God has endured with much patience the vessels of wrath fitted for destruction? [23]And wishing to make known the riches of the glory, what if God bears with the vessels of mercy previously prepared for glory? [24]God has called us, not only Judeans but also people from other nations. [25]As indeed God says in Hosea, "Those who were not my people I will call 'my people,' and those not beloved I will call 'my beloved.'" *(Hos 2.23)* [26]"And in the very place where it was said to them, 'You are not my people,' they will be called 'children of the living God.'" *(Hos 1.10)*

[27]And Isaiah cries out concerning Israel, "Though the number of the descendants of Israel be as the sand of the sea, only the remnant will be saved, [28]for God will make short work of the sentence pronounced upon the world." *(Is 10.22-23)* [29]And as Isaiah predicted, "If the God of hosts had not left us descendants, we would have become like Sodom and been like Gomorrah." *(Is 1.9)* [30]What shall we say, then? That people of other nations who did not pursue righteousness have attained righteousness? a righteousness through faith? [31]But that Israel who pursued a righteousness based on law did not reach that law? [32]Why? Because they did not pursue it through faith, but as if it were based on works. They have stumbled over the stumbling stone, [33]as it is written, "Behold, I

place in Zion a stumbling stone, a rock to overthrow them, and anyone who believes in this One will not be put to shame." *(Is 28.16)*

Chapter X

[1]SISTERS AND BROTHERS, my heart's desire and prayer to God for Israelites is for their salvation. [2]I witness to them that they have a zeal for God, but it is not based on knowledge. [3]For not knowing God's righteousness, and seeking to establish their own, they did not submit to God's righteousness. [4]For Christ is the end of law, and everyone who trusts has righteousness.

[5]Moses writes that the person who practices the righteousness of law will live by it. *(Lev 18.5)* [6]But the righteousness of faith says, "Do not say in your heart, 'Who will ascend into heaven?' *(Deut 30.12)* that is, to bring Christ down; [7]or 'Who will descend into the abyss?' *(Deut 30.13)* that is, to bring Christ up from the dead." [8]But what does it say? "The word is near you, in your mouth and in your heart," *(Deut 30.14)* that is, the word of faith which we proclaim. [9]Because, if you confess with your mouth that Jesus is the Christ and believe in your heart that God raised Christ from the dead, you will be saved. [10]For belief in the heart brings righteousness, and confession in the mouth brings salvation. [11]The scripture says, "No one who believes in Christ shall be put to shame." *(Is 28.16)* [12]For there is no distinction between Judean and Greek. The same one rules over all and the same has riches for all who call upon the one who rules them. [13]For, "Everyone who calls upon the name of God will be saved." *(Joel 2.32)*

[14]But how can people call upon one in whom they have not believed? And how can they believe in one of whom they have never heard? And how can they hear the word if no one proclaims it? [15]And how can people proclaim it unless they are sent? As it is written, "How beautiful are the feet of those who bring good news!" *(Is 52.7)* [16]But not everyone obeyed the gospel, for Isaiah says, "O God, who has believed what they heard from us?" *(Is 53.1)* [17]So faith comes through hearing and hearing comes through the word of Christ. [18]But I ask, have they not heard? Indeed they

have, for, "Their voice has gone out to all the earth, and their words to the ends of the inhabited world." *(Ps 19.4)* [19]Again I ask, did Israel not know? First Moses says, "I will make you jealous of those who are not a nation; with an uninformed nation I will make you angry." *(Deut 32.21)* [20]Then Isaiah is quite bold and says, "I have been found by those who did not seek me; I have shown myself to those who did not inquire for me." *(Is 65.1)* [21]But to Israel, Isaiah says, "All day long I have held out my hands to a disobedient and contrary people." *(Is 65.2)*

Chapter XI

[1]I ASK, THEN, has God rejected the Israelites? Not at all! I myself am an Israelite, a descendant of Abraham and Sarah, a member of the tribe of Benjamin. [2]God has not rejected the chosen people who were foreknown. Do you not know what the scripture says of Elijah, how he pleads with God against Israel? [3]"O God, they have killed your prophets, they have destroyed your altars, I alone am left, and they are trying to kill me." *(I Kgs 19.10,14)* [4]But what is the divine response? "I have reserved for myself seven thousand people who have not bowed the knee to Baal." *(I Kgs 19.18)* [5]So too at the present time there is a remnant, chosen by grace. [6]And if by grace, then no longer by works, otherwise grace would not be grace.

[7]What then? What Israel sought, it failed to obtain. But the chosen ones obtained it. The rest were hardened, [8]as it is written, "God gave them a spirit of stupor, eyes that would not see and ears that would not hear, until this very day." *(Deut 29.4/Is 29.10)* [9]And David says, "Let their eating table become a snare and a trap, a pitfall and a retribution for them. [10]Let their eyes be darkened so that they cannot see, and their backs bent for ever." *(Ps 69.22-23)*

[11]So I ask, have they stumbled in order to fall? Not at all! But through their trespass salvation has come to other nations, to make Israel jealous. [12]Now if their trespass enriches the world, and if their failure enriches other nations, how much more will their wholeness do!

[13]Now I am speaking to you that are not Israelites. Inasmuch then as I am an apostle to other nations, I glorify my ministry [14]in order to provoke jealousy among my kinspeople, and save some of them. [15]For if their rejection reconciles the world, what would their reception be but life from the dead? [16]If the portion offered as first fruit is holy, so is the whole mass; if the root is holy, so are the branches.

[17]But if some of the branches were broken off, and you, a wild olive shoot, were grafted in their place to share the root and richness of the olive tree, [18]do not boast about the branches. If you do boast, remember it is not you that support the root, but the root that supports you. [19]You will say then, "Branches were broken off in order that I might be grafted in." [20]True, they were broken off because of their unbelief, and through faith you remain. So do not be proud, but rather fearful, [21]for if God did not spare the natural branches, neither will God spare you. [22]See then the kindness and the severity of God, severity toward those who have fallen, but kindness to you, provided you continue in God's kindness. Otherwise you too will be cut off. [23]And even the others, if they do not persist in their unbelief, will be grafted in. For God has the power to graft them in again. [24]If you have been cut from what is by nature a wild olive tree, and contrary to nature, grafted into a cultivated olive tree, how much more will these natural branches be grafted back into their own olive tree.

[25]I do not want you to be ignorant of this mystery, my sisters and brothers, so that you will not be conceited. Resistance has come upon part of Israel, until the full number of other people comes in. [26]So all Israel will be saved, as it is written, "The deliverer will come from Zion, and will banish ungodliness from Israel, [27]and this is my covenant with them when I take away their sins." (Is 59.20/Is 27.9) [28]According to the gospel they are, for your sake, enemies of God. But as they are the chosen people they are beloved for the sake of their ancient ones. [29]For the gifts and the call of God are not withdrawn. [30]Just as you were once disobedient to God, but now have received mercy because of their disobedience, [31]so they are now being disobedient in order that by your mercy they also may receive mercy. [32]For God has imprisoned all

people in disobedience, that God may show mercy for all people. [33]O depth of riches, wisdom, and knowledge in God! How inscrutable are God's judgments and ways! [34]For who knows God's mind or who can advise? [35]Or who has given a gift to God that must be returned? [36]All things come from God, exist in God, belong to God. Glory to God forever. *Amen.*

Chapter XII

[1]I BEG YOU THEREFORE, sisters and brothers, through the compassionate love of God, to present your bodies as holy, living offerings, your rational service, pleasing to God. [2]Do not be conformed to this age but be transformed by the renewal of your mind, to prove what is the will of God, what is good and pleasing and perfect.

[3]For I ask, by the grace given to me, everyone among you not to think of yourself more highly than you ought to think, but to think with sober mind, each according to the measure of faith God has assigned you. [4]For as in one body we have many components, and all the components do not have the same function, [5]so we, though many, are one body in Christ, and individually components of the group. [6]We have different gifts given to us according to grace, either prophecy in proportion to our faith, [7]or ministry in our ministering, the teacher in teaching, [8]the one who exhorts in exhortation, the one who shares in simplicity, the leader in diligence, the merciful in cheerfulness.

[9]Let love be genuine. Avoid evil; hold fast to the good. [10]Love one another warmly with familial affection; honor and give preference to one another. [11]Never be sluggish in zeal; be aglow with the spirit; serve God. [12]Rejoice in your hope; be patient when afflicted; be constant in prayer. [13]Contribute to the needs of the saints; practice hospitality.

[14]Bless those who persecute you; bless and do not curse them. [15]Rejoice with those who rejoice; weep with those who weep. [16]Be mindful of equality among you; do not seek exalted positions but attend to the humble; never be conceited. [17]Repay no one evil for evil, but provide good things for all people.

[18]If possible, so far as it depends upon you, live peaceably with everyone. [19]Beloved, never avenge yourselves, but abandon your wrath to God, for it is written that God said, "Vengeance is mine, I will repay." *(Deut 32.35)* [20]But "If your enemy is hungry, give food; if thirsty, give drink; for by so doing you will heap burning coals upon the enemy's head." *(Prov 25.21-22)* [21]Do not be overcome by evil, but overcome evil with good.

Chapter XIII

[1]LET EVERY PERSON be subject to the governing authorities. For there is no authority except from God, and those authorities that exist have been ordained by God. [2]Therefore one who resists the authorities opposes the ordinance of God, and those who oppose it will incur judgment on themselves. [3]For rulers are not a terror to good conduct, but to bad. Would you like to have no fear of authority? Then do what is good, and you will receive praise for it. [4]For the one in authority is God's servant for your own good. But if you do wrong, be afraid, for the ruler does not bear the sword for nothing. As the servant of God the ruler executes God's wrath on the wrongdoer. [5]Therefore one must be subject, not only to avoid God's wrath but also for the sake of conscience. [6]For the same reason you also pay taxes, for the authorities act for God, in constant attendance to this very thing. [7]Pay to all their dues, taxes, to whom taxes are due, tribute to whom tribute is due, fear to whom fear is due, honor to whom honor is due.

[8]Owe no one anything, except love to one another. For one who loves a neighbor has fulfilled the law. [9]The commandments, "You shall not commit adultery, you shall not kill, you shall not steal, you shall not covet, and any other commandment, are summed up in this sentence, "You shall love your neighbor as yourself." [10]Love does no wrong to a neighbor; therefore love fulfills the law.

[11]Besides this, you know what time it is, how it is now the time for you to be wakened from sleep, for salvation is nearer to us now than when we first believed. [12]The night is far gone, and the day is soon to dawn. Therefore let us cast off the works of darkness and put on the weapons of light. [13]Let us conduct ourselves as befits

the day, not in reveling and drunkenness, not in orgies and excesses, not in quarreling and jealousy. [14]But wrap yourself in Christ Jesus and make no provision to gratify the lusts of the flesh.

Chapter XIV

[1]WELCOME THE PERSON who is weak in faith, but not to long discussions of opinion. [2]One person may believe in eating anything, while those weak in faith eat only vegetables. [3]Let not the one who eats despise one who abstains, and let not one who abstains pass judgment on one who eats, for God has welcomed each. [4]Who are you to judge the servant of another? It is before one's own supervisor that one stands or falls. But everyone will stand, for the one who rules us is able to uphold each person.

[5]One person may esteem one day as better than another, while another esteems all days alike. Let all be fully convinced in their own minds. [6]One mindful of a particular day is mindful of God. One also who eats, eats to honor God, and gives thanks to God. One who abstains, abstains to honor God and gives thanks to God. [7]None of us lives to ourselves, nor do we die to ourselves. [8]If we live, we live to God, and if we die, we die to God. So then, whether we live or whether we die, we belong to God. [9]For to this end Christ died and lived again, that Christ might rule over both the dead and the living.   [10]Why do you pass judgment on your brother or sister? Or you, why do you despise your sister or brother? We shall all stand before the judgment seat of God, [11]for it is written, "As I live, says the one who rules, every knee shall bow to me, and every tongue shall give praise to God." *(Is 45.23)* [12]So each of us shall be accountable to God.

[13]Therefore let us no longer judge one another, but rather resolve never to put a stumbling block or hindrance in the way of a sister or brother.

[14]I know and am persuaded by Christ Jesus that nothing is inferior in itself, but it is inferior to any one who believes it to be so. [15]If your brother or sister is being injured by what you eat, you are no longer walking in love. Do not let your food destroy one for whom Christ died. [16]So do not let your good be called evil. [17]For

the rule of God is not in eating and drinking but is righteousness, peace, and joy in the Holy Spirit. [18]The one who thus serves Christ is pleasing to God and approved by people.

[19]Therefore, let us pursue the things that make peace and are constructive for one another. [20]Do not, for the sake of food, destroy the work of God. Everything is indeed clean, but eating things that cause others to fall is evil. [21]It is best not to eat meat, nor drink wine, nor do anything to cause your brother or sister to stumble. [22]Let your own faith be between yourself and God; happy is the one whose approval of anything is not cause for self-condemnation. [23]But one who doubts is condemned for eating because the eating was not an act of faith. For whatever does not proceed from faith is sin.

Chapter XV

[1]WE WHO ARE STRONG ought to bear the failings of the weak, and not please ourselves. [2]Let each of us please our neighbor to build up the neighbor's good. [3]For even Jesus did not please himself, but as it is written, "The reproaches of those who reproached you fell on me." (Ps 69.9) [4]For whatever was written in the past was written for our instruction, that by patience and by the comfort of the writings we might have hope. [5]May the God of patience and comfort keep you mindful of these things with one another, in accord with Christ Jesus, [6]that together you may with one voice glorify the God and source of Jesus Christ whom we serve.

[7]Accept one another, therefore, as Christ has accepted you, for the glory of God. [8]For I tell you that Christ became a minister to the people of the law to show God's truthfulness, in order to confirm the promises given to our ancestors, [9]and in order that people of other nations might glorify the mercy of God. As it is written, "Therefore I will make you known among the nations, and sing praise to your name." (Ps 18.49) [10]And again it is said, "Rejoice, O nations, with God's people." (Deut 32.43) [11]And again, "Praise God, all nations; let all the peoples praise God." (Ps 117.1) [12]And further Isaiah says, "The root of Jesse shall come, one who rises to rule all nations and in whom the nations hope." (Is 11.10) [13]May

the God of Hope fill you with all joy and peace in believing, so that by the power of the Holy Spirit you may overflow with hope.

[14]I myself am convinced that you, my sisters and brothers, are yourselves full of goodness, and filled with all knowledge, so that you can instruct one another. [15]But on some points I have written to you very boldly by way of reminder, because God gave me grace [16]to be a minister of Christ Jesus to other nations, a priestly intermediary of the good news of God, so that the offering of other nations may be acceptable, sanctified by the Holy Spirit. [17]Therefore, in Christ Jesus I have reason to boast of the work of God. [18]For I will not venture to speak of anything except what Christ has brought about through me to achieve obedience from other nations, by word and deed, [19]by the power of signs and wonders, by the power of the Spirit, so that from Jerusalem and as far as Illyricum I have fulfilled the gospel of Christ; [20]thus eagerly striving to evangelize, not where Christ has already been named, lest I build on another person's foundation, [21]but as it is written, "They shall see who have never been told about God's servant and those who have not heard will understand." *(Is 52.15)*

[22]For this reason I have so often been hindered from coming to you. [23]But now, since I no longer have a place in these regions, and since I have wanted for many years to come to you, [24]I hope to see you as I pass through on my journey to Spain, and to have you send me on my way, after I have enjoyed your company for a little. [25]But now I am going to Jerusalem with aid for the saints. [26]For Macedonia and Achaia thought it a good thing to make some contribution for the poor among the saints at Jerusalem. [27]They were pleased to do it, and indeed they are in debt to them, for as other nations have shared in spiritual blessings, they ought also to minister to them in material blessings. [28]Therefore, when I have completed this, and have delivered to them this produce, I shall travel by way of you to Spain; [29]and I know that in coming to you I shall come in the fulness of the blessing of Christ.

[30]Now, brothers and sisters, I beg you, by Jesus Christ whom we serve, and by the love of the Spirit, to strive together with me in prayers to God on my behalf, [31]that I may be delivered from the disobedient in Judea, and that my ministry to Jerusalem may be ac-

ceptable to the saints, ³²so that by God's will I may come to you with joy and be refreshed in your company. ³³The God of peace be with you all. *Amen.*

Chapter XVI

¹NOW I COMMEND to you our sister Phoebe, a minister of the church at Cenchreae, ²that you may receive her in Christ as befits the saints, and stand by her in whatever she may need, for she has been a protector of many and of myself as well.

³Greet Prisca and Aquila, joint workers with me in Christ Jesus, ⁴who risked their necks on my behalf, to whom not only I but also all the churches of the nations give thanks. ⁵Greet also the church in their house.

Greet my beloved Epaenetus, who was the first convert in Asia for Christ.

⁶Greet Mary, who has worked hard among you.

⁷Greet Andronicus and Junias, my kinspeople and prisoners with me; they are notable among the apostles, and were in Christ before me.

⁸Greet Ampliatus, my beloved in Christ.

⁹Greet Urbanus, joint worker with us in Christ, and my beloved Stachys.

¹⁰Greet Apelles, who is approved in Christ.

Greet those who belong to the family of Aristobulus.

¹¹Greet Herodion, my relative.

Greet those in Christ who belong to the family of Narcissus.

¹²Greet Tryphaena and Tryphosa, women who work in Christ.

Greet the beloved Persis, who also worked hard in Christ.

¹³Greet Rufus, chosen in Christ, also his mother and mine.

¹⁴Greet Asyncritus, Phlegon, Hermes, Patrobas, Hermas, and the brothers and sisters who are with them.

¹⁵Greet Philologus, Julia, Nereus and his sister, and Olympas, and all the saints who are with them.

¹⁶Greet one another with a holy kiss. All the churches of Christ greet you.

¹⁷Now I beg you, sisters and brothers, to be on the watch for

those who cause dissensions and obstructions, contrary to the doctrine which you have been taught. Avoid them. [18]For such persons do not serve Christ whom we serve, but they serve their own appetites, and by fair and flattering words they deceive the hearts of naive people. [19]For your obedience is known to all, and I rejoice over you, but I want you to be wise as to what is good and simpletons as to what is evil. [20]The God of peace will soon crush Satan under your feet. The grace of Christ Jesus whom we serve be with you.

[21]Timothy, my companion worker, greets you; as do Lucius, Jason, and Sosipater, my relatives.

[22]I Tertius, the writer of this letter, greet you in Christ.

[23]Gaius, who is host to me and to the whole church, greets you. Erastus, the city treasurer, and our brother Quartus, greet you.

[24]The grace of Jesus Christ whom we serve be with you. *Amen.*

[25]Now to the one God who is able to establish you according to my gospel and the proclamation of Jesus Christ, according to the revelation of the mystery which was hidden for long ages, [26]but is now revealed and through the prophetic writings, according to the command of the eternal God, is made known to all nations, to bring about obedience to the faith, [27]to the only wise God be glory for ever more through Jesus Christ! *Amen.*

The Epistle to the Galatians

Chapter I

[1]PAUL AN APOSTLE—not from humans nor through humanity, but through Jesus Christ and God the Creator, who raised the Christ from the dead—[2]and all the brothers and sisters who are with me,

To the churches of Galatia:

[3]Grace to you and peace from God who cares for all of us and our beloved Jesus Christ whom we serve, [4]who was crucified for our sins to deliver us from the present evil age, according to the will of our God and Creator; [5]to whom be glory forever and ever. *Amen.*

[6]I am amazed that you are so quickly deserting the one who called you by the grace of Christ and are turning to another gospel, [7]which is not really a gospel, but there are some who trouble you and want to pervert the gospel of Christ. [8]But even if I, or an angel from heaven, should proclaim to you a gospel other than what we did proclaim to you, let that person be accursed. [9]As we have said before, so now I say again, if any one proclaims to you a gospel other than that which you received, let that person be accursed.

[10]For now, do I appeal to humans or to God? Or do I seek to please men and women? If I were still pleasing men and women, I should not be a slave of Christ.

[11]I make known to you, brothers and sisters, that the gospel proclaimed by me is not a gospel according to human values. [12]I did not receive it from humans, nor was I taught it, but it came through a revelation of Jesus Christ. [13]For you have heard of my former conduct in Judaism, that I persecuted the church of God violently and tried to destroy it; [14]and I progressed in Judaism beyond many of my contemporaries among my people, so extremely zealous was I for the traditions of my ancestors. [15]But when the one who had set me apart before I was born, and had called me

through the grace of God, ¹⁶was pleased to reveal the Child of God to me, so that I might proclaim Christ among other nations, I did not confer with flesh and blood, ¹⁷nor did I go up to Jerusalem to those who were apostles before me, but I went away into Arabia, and again returned to Damascus.

¹⁸Then after three years I went up to Jerusalem to visit Cephas, and remained with him fifteen days. ¹⁹But I saw none of the other apostles except James, the brother of Jesus. ²⁰(In what I am writing to you, before God, I do not lie!) ²¹Then I went into the regions of Syria and Cilicia. ²²And I was still not known by sight to the churches of Christ in Judea, ²³but they only heard that the one who had been persecuting them was now proclaiming the faith he had tried to destroy. ²⁴And they glorified God because of me.

Chapter II

¹THEN AFTER FOURTEEN YEARS I went up again to Jerusalem with Barnabas, taking Titus along with me. ²I went there because of a revelation; and privately, before the reputed leaders, I set forth the gospel which I proclaim among the other nations to assure that I was not, and am not, running for nothing.

³And even Titus who was with me, though he was a Greek, was not compelled to be circumcised. ⁴Yet false followers were secretly brought in; they sneaked in to spy on our freedom which we have in Christ Jesus, and they wished to bring us into slavery. ⁵But we did not yield in subjection to them even for a moment, that the truth of the gospel might continue with you.

⁶From those so-called leaders, (what they were makes no difference to me; God does not attend to appearances) those, I say, who were of repute had nothing to add to my gospel. ⁷On the contrary, when they saw that I had been entrusted with the gospel to other nations, just as Peter had been entrusted with the gospel to the Israelites, ⁸and that the one God who worked through Peter as the apostle to the traditionalists worked through me also for other peoples, ⁹and knowing that grace was given to me, James and Cephas and John, the so-called pillars, gave to me and Barnabas the hand of partnership that we should go to other nations and they to

the Israelites. ^{10}Only they would have us remember the poor, the very thing which I was eager to do.

^{11}But when Cephas came to Antioch I opposed him to his face, because he stood condemned. ^{12}For until certain people came from James, Cephas ate with people of other nations; but after they came, he withdrew and separated himself, fearing the advocates of straict legalism. ^{13}And with Cephas the rest of the Judeans also dissembled, so that even Barnabas was carried away by their insincerity. ^{14}But when I saw that they were not straightforward about the truth of the gospel, I said to Cephas in front of them all, "If you, though a Judean, live like an alien and not like a Judean, how can you compel people of other nations to live like Judeans?"

^{15}We ourselves are legally born Judeans and not alien sinners, ^{16}yet we know that a person is not justified by works of the law but rather through faith in Jesus Christ. Even we have believed in Christ Jesus, in order to be justified by faith in Christ, and not by works of the law; because no person can be justified by works of the law. ^{17}But if, in our endeavor to be justified in Christ, we ourselves were found to be sinners, is Christ then a servant of sin? Impossible! ^{18}But if I reconstruct those things which I destroyed, then I myself become a transgressor. ^{19}For I, through law, died to law, that I might live to God. ^{20}I have been co-crucified with Christ; it is no longer I who live, but Christ lives in me; and the life I now live in the flesh, I live by faith in the Child of God, who loved me and lived and died for me.

^{21}I do not abolish the grace of God; for if righteousness comes through law, then Christ died for nothing.

Chapter III

^{1}O FOOLISH GALATIANS! Who bewitched you? You, before whose eyes the crucified Jesus Christ was portrayed! ^{2}I want to learn from you only this: Did you receive the spirit by works of the law, or by hearing with faith? ^{3}Are you so foolish? Having begun with the spirit, are you now made perfect by human effort? ^{4}Did you suffer so many things for nothing? Is it really for nothing? ^{5}Does the one who supplies the spirit to you and works miracles among you do so because you work by law, or because you hear with faith?

⁶Thus Abraham and Sarah "trusted God, and it was counted as righteousness." *(Gen 15:6)* ⁷So you see that it is people of faith who are the children of Abraham and Sarah. ⁸And the scripture, foreseeing that God would justify other nations by faith, proclaimed the good news before hand to Sarah and Abraham, saying, "In you shall all the nations be blessed." *(Gen 12:3)* ⁹So then, those who are people of faith are blessed with Abraham and Sarah who had faith.

¹⁰Now all those who live by works of the law are under a curse, for it is written, "Cursed is everyone who does not live according to all the things written in the book of the law, and do them." *(Deut 27:26)* ¹¹Now it is clear that no one is justified before God by the law, for "The just person lives by faith." *(Hab 2:4)* ¹²But the law does not rest on faith, for "anyone who acts by laws shall live by law." *(Lev 18:5)* ¹³Christ redeemed us from the curse of the law, by becoming a curse for us, for it is written, "Cursed be everyone who hangs on a tree," *(Deut 21:23)* ¹⁴that in Christ Jesus the blessing of Sarah and Abraham might come upon all nations that we might receive the promise of the spirit through faith.

¹⁵To give a human example, brothers and sisters: No one annuls or makes additions to a covenant, once it has been ratified. ¹⁶Now the promises were made to Sarah and Abraham and their descendant. It does not say, "and to descendants," referring to many; but referring to one, "and to your descendant," which is Christ. ¹⁷This is what I say: The law, which came four hundred and thirty years afterward, does not annul a covenant previously ratified by God, so as to abolish the promise. ¹⁸For if the inheritance is according to law, it is no longer by promise; but God gave it to Abraham and Sarah by promise.

¹⁹Why then the law? It was added because of transgressions, until the descendant should come to whom the promise had been made; and it was ordained by angels through a mediator. ²⁰Now a mediator implies another person, but God is one.

²¹Is the law then against the promises of God? Impossible! For if law had been given which could give life, then righteousness

would really be by the law. [22]But the scripture imprisoned all under sin, so that the promise in Jesus Christ might be given by faith to those who believe.

[23]But before faith came, we were imprisoned and guarded under the law, until faith should be revealed. [24]So the law was our teacher, until Christ came that we might be justified by faith. [25]But now that faith has come, we are no longer under a tutor.

[26]Through faith in Christ Jesus you are all sons and daughters of God. [27]For as many of you as were baptized into Christ have put on Christ. [28]There cannot be Judean and Greek, there cannot be slave and free, there cannot be male and female, for you are all one in Christ Jesus. [29]If you are Christ's, then you are descendants of Sarah and Abraham, heirs according to promise.

Chapter IV

[1]BUT I SAY THAT THE HEIR, as long as the heir is an infant, is no better than a slave, though owner of everything. [2]The child is under guardians and trustees until the time previously set by the parents. [3]So also we, when we were infants, we were slaves to the principles of the world. [4]But when the time had fully come, God sent forth the descendant, born of woman, born under the law, [5]to redeem those who were under the law, so that we might receive adoption as daughters and sons. [6]And because you are sons and daughters, God has sent forth the spirit of the Child of God into our hearts, crying, "My loving parent! Source of my being!" [7]So through God you are no longer a slave but a daughter or son, and if daughter or son, then an heir.

[8]Formerly, when you did not know God, you served as slaves to things that by nature are not gods; [9]but now that you know God, or rather are known by God, how can you turn back again to those weak and poor principles, or want to slave for them again? [10]Yet you commemorate certain days, months, seasons, and years! [11]I fear for you, that I have labored among you for nothing.

[12]Sisters and brothers, I beg you, be as I am, for I also am like you. You did me no wrong; [13]you know it was because of the body's weakness that I proclaimed the good news to you earlier.

¹⁴Though my condition was a trial to you, you neither scorned nor despised me, but received me as a messenger of God, as Christ Jesus.   ¹⁵What has become of the joy you felt? For I witness to you that, if possible, you would have gouged out your eyes and given them to me. ¹⁶Have I then become your enemy because I tell you the truth? ¹⁷Others are zealous for you, not for good, but because they want you to be separated from us so that you may be zealous for them. ¹⁸In a good cause it is always good to be zealous, and not only when I am present with you. ¹⁹My little children, for whom I am again in birth labor until Christ be formed in you, ²⁰I wished to be present with you just now and to change my speech, for I am perplexed about you.

²¹Tell me, you that want to be under law, do you not hear the law? ²²For it is written that Abraham had two sons, one of the maidservant and one of the free woman. ²³But the child of the maidservant was born according to human contrivance, the child of the free woman through the promise. ²⁴Now this is an allegory; these are two covenants. The one from Mount Sinai*, bearing children to slavery, is Hagar. ²⁵Now Hagar is Mount Sinai in Arabia, and corresponds to the present Jerusalem, for she serves as a slave with her children. ²⁶But the Jerusalem that is above is free, and is our mother. ²⁷For it is written, "Rejoice, sterile one that does not bear; break forth and shout, you that are not in labor, for the woman alone has more children than the one who has the husband." *(Is 54.1)*

²⁸But you, sisters and brothers, like Isaac, are children of the promise. ²⁹As in that time, children born according to human contrivance persecuted children born according to the spirit, so it is now. ³⁰But what does scripture say? "Cast out the maidservant and her child; for the child of the maidservant shall not inherit with the child of the free woman." *(Gen 21:10)* ³¹So brothers and sisters, we are not children of the maidservant but of the free woman.

Chapter V

¹FOR FREEDOM CHRIST FREED US; stand firm therefore, and do not submit again to a yoke of slavery.

*The law was given at Mt. Sinai.

²Now look, I Paul say to you that if you take on part of the old covenant such as circumcision for males, Christ will be of no value to you. ³I testify again that every male who receives the ceremonial circumcision is bound to keep the whole law. ⁴If you claim justification by the law, you are cut off from Christ. You have fallen from grace. ⁵For through the spirit, by faith, we eagerly expect the hope of righteousness. ⁶In Christ Jesus neither ceremonial nor unceremonial is of any avail, but faith working through love. ⁷You were running well; who prevented you from being persuaded by the truth? ⁸This persuasion is not from the one who called you. ⁹A little yeast leavens the whole lump. ¹⁰I trust in God that you will not think otherwise, but the one who is troubling you will bear the judgment, whoever that person may be. ¹¹But if I, brothers and sisters, still preach legalism, why am I still persecuted? In that case the scandal of the cross has been annulled. ¹²I wish those who unsettle you would mutilate themselves!

¹³You were called for freedom, sisters and brothers; only do not use your freedom for gratification of the flesh, but through love be servants of one another. ¹⁴For the whole law is fulfilled in one word, "You shall love your neighbor as yourself." *(Lev 19.18)* ¹⁵But if you bite and devour one another, take care that you are not destroyed by one another.

¹⁶I say this: Walk in the spirit, and you will never act out of physical desire. ¹⁷For physical desires are contrary to spirit, and desires of the spirit are contrary to the physical; for these are opposed to each other, to prevent you from doing whatever you wish. ¹⁸But if you are led by the spirit, you are not under the law.

¹⁹Now the works of the flesh are obvious: fornication, uncleanness, lewdness, ²⁰idolatry, sorcery, enmities, strife, jealousy, angers, rivalry, dissension, factions, ²¹envy, drunkenness, carousing, and the like. I warn you, as I warned you before, that those who practice such things will not inherit the realm of God. ²²But the fruit of the spirit is love, joy, peace, patience, kindness, goodness, faithfulness, ²³meekness, and self-control; against such there is no law. ²⁴Those who belong to Christ Jesus have crucified the flesh with its passions and its lusts.

²⁵If we live in the spirit, let us also walk in the spirit. ²⁶Let us

not become conceited, nor provoke one another, nor envy.

Chapter VI

[1]SISTERS AND BROTHERS, if anyone is overcome by some sin, you who are spiritual should restore that person in a spirit of meekness, and watch yourself, for you too may be tempted. [2]Carry one another's burdens and so fulfill the law of Christ. [3]For if any one pretends to be something, while actually being nothing, that person is self-deceived. [4]But let each one prove his or her own work, and then the boast will be within each person and not in some other. [5]Each person will carry her or his own load.

[6]Let those who are taught the word share all good things with those who teach.

[7]Do not be deceived; God is not mocked. Whatever a person plants, the same will also be harvested. [8]For those who plant their own human ways will harvest human corruption; but those who plant the spirit will from the spirit harvest eternal life. [9]And let us not grow weary of doing good, for in the proper season we shall collect the harvest, if we do not give up. [10]So then, while we have time, let us do good to all people, and most of all to the members of the family of faith.

[11]See with what large letters I write to you by my own hand. [12]Those who want to look good in the human way would compel male persons to be circumcised only so that they will not be persecuted for the cross of Christ. [13]For even those males who receive the ritual circumcision do not themselves keep the law, but they want to have other males circumcised so that they may boast of success.

[14]But for me, I cannot boast except in the cross of Jesus Christ whom we serve, through whom the world has been crucified to me, and I to the world.

[15]Neither ceremonies nor lack of ceremonies counts for anything. What counts is new creation. [16]Peace and mercy be upon all who walk by this rule, upon God's Israel.

[17]Henceforth let no one trouble me; for I bear on my body the mark of Jesus.

[18]The grace of Jesus Christ whom we serve be with your spirit, brothers and sisters . *Amen.*